33 Gems ♦ Wisdom for Living Pieces

33 GEMS
Wisdom for Living Pieces of Life's Puzzle

AASBEA Publishers
Gems of Wisdom Consulting, Inc.

1629 K Street, NW, Suite 300
Washington, DC 20006-1602
Email: info@gemsofwisdomconsulting.com
Web: www.gemsofwisdomconsulting.com
Phone: Sharon T. Freeman, Ph.D. (202) 699-2368

Freeman, Sharon T., et.al.

33 Gems ✦ Wisdom for Living Pieces of Life's Puzzle

    1. Self-help/ Self- improvement
    2. Life stories
    3. Inspiration and motivation

I. Freeman, Sharon T., et.al.   II. Title.

© 2018 Sharon T. Freeman, Ph.D., et.al.
All rights reserved.
Printed in the United States of America.

ISBN 978-0-9816885-5-8 (Trade Paper)

All rights reserved. Printed in the United States of America. No part of this publication may be reproduced, stored in retrieval system or transmitted in any form or by any means, electronic, mechanical, photocopying, recording or otherwise, without the written permission of the publisher.

Publisher:

AASBEA Publishers

All American Small Business Exporters Association, Inc. (AASBEA)
GEMS OF WISDOM CONSULTING, INC.

1629 K Street, NW, Suite 300
Washington, DC 20006-1602

Email: info@gemsofwisdomconsulting.com
Web: www.gemsofwisdomconsulting.com
Phone: Sharon T. Freeman, Ph.D. (202) 699-2368

ORDERING INFORMATION:
Amazon
and
www.gemsofwisdomconsulting.com

Cover design and Graphic layout by Creative Services, Chester, Maryland

Table of Contents

Essayist Acknowledgment & Appreciation vi

Introduction vii

Politics and Activism

Gem ✦1:   This I know for sure: *In order to effectively manage change and to build bridges that lead to successful outcomes, you must seek to be informed, build coalitions, and respectfully acknowledge the differences that exist in our society.* (**Ike Leggett**) 1

Gem ✦2:   This I know for sure: *The game of Scrabble contains a microcosm of life's important lessons.* (**Cheryl Kagan**) 6

Gem ✦3:   This I know for sure: *Black owned media must survive!* (**Denise Rolark-Barnes**) 11

Gem ✦4:   This I know for sure: *It's important to be politically active and to hold candidates to the highest standard of integrity.* (**Paul Bessel**) 17

Spirituality, Society & Sustainability

Gem ✦5:   This I know for sure: *GOD "SHAPE-d" me to do what I am doing to help minority firms bridge the access-to-capital gap.* (**Stanley Tucker**) 21

Gem ✦6:   *This I know for sure: God is real and His word is true.* (**Doyle Mitchell**) 28

Gem ✦7:   This I know for sure: *God has given me the ability to discern the good and bad in life and to harness its lessons to turn every obstacle into a stepping stone for reaching higher goals in my business and life.* (**Stacy Trammell**) 32

Gem ✦8:   This I know for sure: *Success, growth, and meaning in life come from human connections that one must always cultivate.* (**Shelton "Shelly" Williams**) 38

Gem ✦9:   This I know for sure: *Consumption at current levels represents a threat, locally and globally, to the natural resources on which we depend and therefore to the wider socio-economic system.* (**Sandra Taylor**) 41

Entrepreneurship

Gem ✦10:   This I know for sure: *The impossible may just be possible.* (**Robert Wallace**) 45

Gem ✦11: This I know for sure: *Sometimes it appears that entrepreneurial success comes out of nowhere, but that's rarely the case; it more commonly develops on a foundation of learning, prior experience, and firsthand observation.* (**Roger Mariner**).................................**49**

Gem ✦12: This I know for sure: *Always Be Creating Value. (ABCV)* (**Gigi Wang**)..**53**

Gem ✦13: This I know for sure: *We have needs and wants... I enjoy building off the magic that comes when they intersect.* (**Warren Brown**)...**57**

Career and Self-Development

Gem ✦14: This I know for sure: *You must find your passion(s) and ways to pursue them. Hopefully, you can make them your profession, but if not, you can integrate them into your life.* (**Lauri Fitzpegado**)..**60**

Gem ✦15: This I know for sure: *You must learn how to learn before you can master yourself and your fate.* (**Sharon Freeman**)............**64**

Gem ✦16: This I know for sure: *Everybody needs to travel through life with a "road dog."* (**Norman Johnson**)...............................**68**

Gem ✦17: This I know for sure: *The Right Plant in the Right Place OR It's Not All about You.* (**Bruce McGee**)..............................**72**

Gem ✦18: This I know for sure: *You must always be true to yourself and let your inner light shine.* (**Shara Dae Howard**)............**76**

Thriving, Health, &Family

Gem ✦19: This I know for sure: *If you want to thrive in life and over its long haul, you must design yourself to do that!* (**Betty Smith**).........**80**

Gem ✦20: This I know for sure: *For many Americans diagnosed with a serious illness such as cancer, navigating their journey through our fragmented health care system can be daunting, fraught with missteps and unclear directions, but they can make the system work for them.* (**CJ Hunter**)..**83**

Gem ✦21: This I know for sure: *Each of us has the opportunity to improve on our parents' influence, if we can only muster the tremendous courage and insight it takes to do so.* (**John Rich**).....................**88**

Gem ✦22: This I know for sure: *Resilience is seated in the depth of our connections to ourselves and others.* (**Lisa McClennon**)...............**92**

33 Gems ✦ Wisdom for Living Pieces of Life's Puzzle   v

Global Perspectives

Gem ✦23: This I know for sure: *I was born in a New York City hospital in 1952, yet the essence of me was began long before that.* (**David Robinson**) 96

Gem ✦24: This I know for sure: *As you travel on life's highway, it's important to serve and help others, and not just yourself.* (**Mattie Sharpless**) 100

Gem ✦25: This I know for sure: *Career success is largely due to a sustained level of readiness for the next challenge and seizing opportunities with unwavering confidence.* (**David Cutting**) 104

Gem ✦26: This I know for sure: *No matter what objective you seek to accomplish in international development, achieving success is always about the people you get to work with.* (**Larry Hearn**) 108

Gem ✦27: This I know for sure: *You have to come to a fundamental understanding of yourself before you can authentically support the development of others.* (**Sarah Phillips**) 112

Gem ✦28: This I know for sure: *Understanding and accepting diversity has made me a better person and more productive throughout my career, by fostering greater collaboration among my many colleagues.* (**Juan Albert**) 116

Gem ✦29: This I know for sure: *It was my inability to successfully plan my life that landed me in destinations that were exactly where I should have been.* (**Jim Harvey**) 120

Art, Crafts & Music

Gem ✦30: This I know for sure: *Music is a healing force in the universe.* (**" Baba Doc" Lenny Gibbs**) 123

Gem ✦31: This I know for sure: *Creativity can be a pathway to joy.* (**Cynthia Farrell**) 128

Gem ✦32: This I know for sure: *Creative endeavors are much more than hobbies; they feed our souls, relationships, and pocketbooks.* (**Jacqueline Ganim de Falco**) 131

Gem ✦33: This I know for sure: *When you are trying to make it in the music business you can't rush the process.* (**Rudy Monteiro**) 135

Afterword:

Negash Gebre 139

Acknowledgment and Appreciation

A note of deep gratitude to all of the 33 essayists in the book. Your wisdom and frankness is valuable and illuminating and will no doubt serve as a point of reference for readers for many years to come.

Thank you essayists:

"Baba Doc" Gibbs
Betty Smith
Bruce McGee
Cheryl Kagan
CJ Hunter
Cynthia Farrell
David Cutting
David Robinson
Denise Rolark-Barnes
Doyle Mitchell
Gigi Wang
Ike Leggett
Jacqueline Gamin-DeFalco
Jim Harvey
John Rich
Juan Albert
Larry Hearn
Lauri Fitzpegado
Lisa McClennon
Mattie Sharpless
Norman Johnson
Paul Bessel
Robert Wallace
Roger Mariner
Rudy Monteiro
Sandra Taylor
Sarah Phillips
Shara Dae Howard
Sharon Freeman
Shelton "Shelly" Williams
Stacy Trammell
Stanley Tucker
Warren Brown

... and Negash Gebre (Afterword)

Introduction

Life is puzzling. The collection of 33 essays in this book share wisdom about how some of the "pieces" of the puzzle are being lived by 33 essayists who are from many walks of life.

Why 33 essays? The number 33 has profound meaning in many walks of life, both biblically and mythologically. Among the claims of its significance is that "…it resonates with the energies of compassion, blessings, inspiration, honesty, discipline, bravery, and courage." This definition captures the spirit and messages of many of the essays in this book.

Each essay begins with the words: *"This I Know for Sure…"* and then provides vignettes of the author's life and formative experiences, and explains how s/he came to "know this for sure." Some of the essays convey how their authors made something out of nothing; some show how they multiplied their existing good fortunes; while others present a snapshot of the beginning or halfway stages of a life's journey. No two stories are alike, but each is heartfelt and caused its author to deeply mine his or her "gems of wisdom" in order to select important lessons learned from the author's treasure trove. Collectively, the shared wisdom can be uploaded into the great cloud in the sky and downloaded into your personal navigable roadmap for life.

No matter what stage you are at in your life, no matter what profession you are in, or how successful or otherwise you might be in your life at the point of reading this book, these stories will enlighten and inspire you, and demonstrate that it's always possible to piece together a life of happiness and self-fulfillment in the grand puzzle of life. Sometimes, the piece of the puzzle you have been handed is in an odd shape and doesn't seem to fit in, but ultimately through trial and error, and personal growth and development, you resize it and make it fit in. This is a book about how people put their *heart, souls, and minds* into reshaping, resizing, and repurposing their pieces of the puzzle to contribute to "the whole" in ways that made their lives and those of others more rewarding.

The "gems of wisdom" shared in this book are from people whose voices may otherwise have not been heard, *but are as valuable and tradable as any currency in the world*. As you read the 33 essays in this book, note the common themes that emerge such as the importance of having mentors, of staying true to yourself, and of the need to make lemonade out of lemons.

Each story was written without knowledge of the others, yet when you boil them down to their essence, many strike the same notes and sing the same songs, despite the differences in the authors' backgrounds, races, religious persuasions, ages, stages of career, and political outlooks. Importantly, they convey the *"us-ness of us"* and that in life…"we must have something to look up to; something to look forward to; and something to chase!"

It is clear from reading the essays that some of the ingredients for how to successfully navigate our lives are common to us all, while others aren't, which is why it's important to learn from each other; we all have our "secret sauce" that we can add to the mix. If you are interested in adding your own "secret sauce" ingredients for the next series, please be in touch on our Amazon page. Enjoy!

Sharon T. Freeman, Ph.D.
Essayist/ Author/ Publisher/Entrepreneur

GEM 1

This I know for sure:
To effectively manage change and to build bridges that lead to successful outcomes, you must seek to be informed, build coalitions, and respectfully acknowledge the differences that exist in our society.

Change is not easy, and it's particularly challenging when it's rapid and all-encompassing. How we communicate with each other in society, how we manage our businesses and social lives, and how we are educated — all are impacted by rapid technological developments and their adoption.

In most cases, our ability to make changes in our routines is greater than our understanding of the meaning of such changes and their true impacts. Our saving grace in this process is, perhaps, only each other. As human beings, we must figure out how to reach one another and recognize that all of us face the same challenges, not just in one county or jurisdiction, but throughout the world. We each walk a mile in each other's shoes.

Collectively, some of our greatest challenges today, in my view, are in three areas: social interactions and the ability to calibrate them correctly; economic and work relations and getting that right; and in government and politics, which is perhaps the most challenging.

Despite the obvious pressures that prevail throughout society, many believe and expect the government can properly manage the change. However, government is as impacted, or perhaps even more impacted, by the forces of change than any other segment of society. In addition to wanting government to be the change agent, we also believe it should take on the role of being the main representative of the hearts, minds, and souls of the people. For instance, when we had a black president for eight years, an aspect of the pride many felt in the nation was that President Obama "represented" our post-racial views and selves. We wanted to believe this, and, in some respects, it was true.

When I first ran for public office in 1986 in Montgomery County, we were a long way from that ideal, however. At that time, we had never elected a person of color to any countywide political office. Even today, other than myself, this has not happened, and the county has over 1.1 million residents, 17% of which are African Americans.

Indeed, when I initially campaigned, my supporters and I were so afraid of a negative reaction to my photograph on the campaign literature that we eliminated it; it was that unprecedented to have a black person run for public office in the county.

After I won the primary, and while campaigning in the general election, I was standing outside of the Metro stop in Friendship Heights (a mostly white area) handing out flyers, now with my photograph on it. An elderly white gentleman, who at first accepted the flyer, returned it to me and said, "Sorry, but I don't vote in Washington, D.C." He thought that I must have been running for office in the black area of Washington, D.C. and that, somehow, I was on the wrong side of the Metro station at Western Avenue.

Yes, my decision to "throw my hat in the ring" was bold, audacious, and unprecedented – and I hadn't expected to do it. In fact, I believed that I was the person best suited to assist and support others who would want to run for office. However, it seemed to many that my background, leadership experience, and community advocacy made me the ideal person to finally break the color barrier in Montgomery County. I had previously created an organization that sought to raise the awareness of minorities about important matters in the county and encourage them to get involved in local politics. Despite my best efforts in the latter regard, no minorities would run; it was just too costly, and the odds did not favor a successful campaign. At the time, the percentage of minorities in every ethnic category was very low: for example, the African American population was about 6%.

In the end, I was persuaded to run by my good friend, the late Roscoe Nix, who said, "Ike, if you won't do it, who will? You are our best hope." So, reluctantly, I decided to run.

Many factors were against me, such as the fact that I wasn't even from the county, I had grown up in the "Jim Crow" south, and I had come from a very humble background with twelve siblings. However, I also knew that I had some assets, chief among which was my willingness to do the hard work involved in running for office in such a vast geographical area that is one of the wealthiest communities in America (meaning that there are many with substantial backing and wealth). Lacking a "built in" constituency, I had to create one by knocking on many doors, staying up late to strategize, and forming many strategic alliances. Once I put my heart and mind into it, for me, "failure was not an option."

What I was sure of was my knowledge of the county and its many issues. I also knew that I was aligned with the majority view on the matters that were most important to the voters. In addition, and most importantly, I believed that when I came face to

GEM 1

face with the potential voters, I could convince them that I was the right person for the job because of my commitment, education, and collaborative approach. This has remained the case through all my elections. Despite not being an outwardly gregarious political person with a "glad-handler" style, what I am known for is my civility and leadership. This, coupled with a belief in my integrity and competence allowed me to win each of my seven election campaigns by large margins.

The same factors that enabled me to win elections were the same that enabled me to be effective in the job. It boils down to ensuring that your constituency sees themselves in you; sees their priorities in your agenda; and believes that their voices are being heard. When you are on this solid ground, it's possible to take bold actions. For instance, I led the county in investing a billion dollars in affordable housing that leveraged $4 billion from the private sector; it resulted in creating and preserving 63,000 affordable housing units. This would never have happened if it was thought to be just "my agenda." Instead, I made it "our" agenda. The same applies to some of "our" other major initiatives: from building 23,000 classrooms, to the unprecedented infrastructure improvements we made during one of the nation's worst recessions. The county now has the highest financial reserves in its history, our budgets are sustainable, and we have maintained a triple A-bond rating, the longest consecutive rating at this level for any county in the country. None of these accomplishments were easy, and the path to success was on winding and zig-zagged roads. The important thing is to recognize that you must be patient, collaborative, transparent, strategic, and get everybody on board in feeling that these are "our" initiatives.

Unfortunately, even today when you are black and in a key leadership role, undue attention must be paid to ensuring that everyone knows that you are advocating for the common good; it cannot just be in the interest of the minority group of which you are a member. Even though the interests of the minority group are often the same as those of the majority, this cannot be merely asserted; it has to be carefully and skillfully woven into the process of collaboration and negotiation whereby everyone comes to that same conclusion.

As I near the end of my third term as Montgomery County Executive and reflect on how I got to where I am, three things stand out: First and foremost, I hear my mother's voice and sage advice from childhood saying, "Son, as a black person, you have to work twice as hard." I believed her and have always acted accordingly. Her second most emphatic message underscored the importance of education, and I listened to her on that and followed her advice. However, her most important advice was to have a solid moral and ethical foundation, and this, too, became my mantra.

GEM 1

I have come to the realization over the years that while it's all well and good to be educated and to possess knowledge, it's not enough. I saw during my years as a law school professor, for instance, that some students are extremely knowledgeable, but they can't put it into production; they simply know facts. Conversely, I have seen many who are both knowledgeable and able to put their knowledge into production, but they try to produce the wrong thing because they lack a moral compass and end up in jail. The prisons are full of brilliant and knowledgeable people who lack a moral foundation.

As we are each called on to manage changes in our lives, my advice is to endeavor to turn deficits into assets and to seek out knowledge and apply it with integrity. When you become effective and adept at this, those who oppose you will become the ones in the "minority."

GEM 1

Gem 1 Essayist: Ike Leggett

From his roots in the hardscrabble poverty of then-segregated Louisiana, Ike Leggett has built a record of public service marked by conviction to principle, leadership, and a willingness to take on tough fights and make hard choices.

In 2006, Leggett won the Democratic Party primary for Montgomery County Executive with 61 percent of the vote. Then, in November of that same year, he was elected the first African American County Executive. He was overwhelmingly reelected in 2010 and 2014. Isiah Leggett served four terms on the County Council.

Born in Texas, Leggett was raised in small-town Alexandria, Louisiana, where he grew up as the seventh of 12 children in a four-room house without indoor plumbing. While studying at Southern University, Leggett was elected student body president, commanded the Reserve Officer Training Corps cadets, and was a campus and community leader in the struggle for civil rights. In that connection, a young Leggett twice met the Rev. Dr. Martin Luther King, Jr.

He holds four higher education degrees: Bachelor of Arts from Southern University, Master of Arts and Juris Doctorate degrees from Howard University, and a Master of Laws from George Washington University. Ike Leggett graduated from Southern University in 1967 as a Distinguished Military Graduate. In 1981, he was selected as the Southern University Outstanding Alumni. He finished first in his class from Howard University Law School, graduating Magna Cum Laude. In 1985, Leggett received the Outstanding Alumni Award from Howard University Law School.

Leggett served as a Captain in the United States Army. His tour of duty in the Vietnam War earned him the Bronze Star Medal, the Vietnam Service, and Vietnam Campaign Medals. In 1977, Ike Leggett was selected as a White House Fellow under President Jimmy Carter. He served as a Professor of Law at the Howard University Law School from 1975 - 2006.

GEM 2

This I know for sure:
The game of Scrabble contains a microcosm all of life's important lessons.

In addition to my day job, (serving as the State Senator for District 17 in Montgomery County) I am a nationally ranked Scrabble player. I find playing Scrabble is an escape that provides a treasure trove of reminders about the frailties, challenges, and opportunities in life. While there are many lessons I have learned from it, I am sharing ten below that capture some of the most important ones.

Lesson #1: A significant part of success is based on luck.
Draw seven tiles from the Scrabble bag. They will launch you toward success or frustration, depending on the mix of vowels and consonants and your ability to rearrange them to fit on the board.

In some ways, I drew a good initial mix from the bag of life. I grew up in an upper-middle-class neighborhood and was educated in one of the nation's best public school systems. Neither I, nor anyone in my immediate family, had any significant mental or physical health problems. However, that picture doesn't capture the rifts and abusive behavior that began before my parents' divorce. My childhood was a challenge in the midst of blessings.

Lesson #2: It's how you manage your rack.
In a recent tournament, I was discouraged by my mix of seven letters: ACCSTT?. Examining the board, rotating the tiles and thinking creatively with the blank (wild card) tile, however, led me to discover TACTiCS and earn the 50-point bonus for playing all seven tiles in one word.

When things were miserable at home, I simply rearranged my tiles. I found solace, friendship and affirmation at school and at work. By escaping to the student government, the school play, babysitting and a part-time job at Sears, I was able to create several alternative families.

Lesson #3: Challenging unethical behavior is your responsibility.
There's one competitor I dislike playing. Her scoring is frequently wrong – and is inevitably in her favor. She regularly plays "phonies" and seems surprised when I challenge them. Unfortunately, I challenge her too often and have thereby forfeited more turns than I'd like to admit. Still, I want her to know that I'm vigilant and won't easily let something slip by.

GEM 2

Many of us are lucky enough to work with people we like and trust. Sometimes, however, we witness or experience actions, decisions or statements that are simply wrong. Whether it's the latest #MeToo sexual harassment incident, knowledge of fraudulent behavior or knowing that a friend is misrepresenting their background on their resume, it's our obligation to speak up and call it out.

Lesson #4: Be conscious of what you leave behind.

In Scrabble, it's not just about the word(s) you play, but about the "leave." If you play four tiles and leave three "I's" in your rack, you're setting yourself up for failure for the next several turns.

Similarly, in life it's not just about what you do while you're here, but what continues after you're gone. What's your legacy? I'm amazed by the number of smart friends who don't have either a last will and testament or a living will, for instance. Let's face it, it's unlikely that you're indifferent to who takes custody of your child or how your assets will be distributed, so why leave it to chance?

In addition to articulating how you'd like your resources to be divided among your loved ones, are you setting aside funds for groups and causes you already support? Even tithing 10% of your assets could make a significant difference for a local nonprofit organization. Whether you are passionate about the arts, homelessness, climate change, gun control or public radio, your dollars will go further and make a difference in a way that an extra chunk steered toward a child, friend or the well-funded endowment at your *alma mater* could never achieve.

Lesson #5: Sometimes, you have to take big risks.

In Scrabble, there may be a fabulous word you've found ... but you're not sure whether it's valid. Do you take a conservative route and find a safer move? Or, do you take a chance and play a (possible or definite) phony? If the word is challenged, it's removed from the board and you lose both your points and your turn. If it's not challenged, it plays!

Our lives offer opportunities to take risks. It could be a new job, a new relationship, talking to a stranger, picking up a new hobby, sampling foreign foods or investing your savings in a start-up business. I fervently believe that I am only on this planet for a finite period of time. I don't know how or when my life will end, but I do control what I do with the years I'm here. I believe in living each day to the fullest, taking risks and experimenting with new things and new people!

GEM 2

Lesson #6: Know when it's time to give up and move forward.

Sometimes, no amount of rotating seven tiles and perusing the Scrabble board will reveal a decent play. In those cases (and sometimes even after playing off a few tiles in the hopes of drawing a better mix) it's wise to give up. Exchanging tiles means losing a turn, so it's not something to do lightly.

In life, it's sometimes the right choice to leave a romantic relationship, a job or a friendship. I struggled within my marriage for several years. I still call David "my beloved ex" for a good reason. We loved (and still love) each other. Our total trust in each other, our shared life experiences and our mutual values formed a strong basis for our relationship.

However, there were significant aspects that weren't working. Even couples' counseling didn't help us to make the changes that might have saved us. After a month apart while I visited Paris (pondering the decision whether to split up), we decided to separate. David helped me locate a new apartment and even helped me move. My lawyer was incredulous at the lack of acrimony or dispute in our split. Five years later, we still talk a couple of times each week, have keys to each other's homes and celebrate together on each other's birthdays. I know that if either of us were in real trouble the other would immediately drop everything to help.

"Trading in" my marriage was a really hard decision, but I believe that it was the right decision for us both.

Lesson #7: Don't get discouraged. Keep your head in the game.

A Scrabble buddy and I were comparing notes after a tournament. Neither of us had done terribly well, but we were both exuberant. We got to stretch our minds, meet new people, get "off the grid" and have a fun day. Not everything will go your way; there will be setbacks. Count on it. But, if you can hold on for the next adventure, success may be waiting!

In my political life, I have had many victories. My first campaign, for the Maryland House of Delegates, was a ten-way race. In addition to the two incumbents, (we have three-member districts) there were two formerly elected officials: the son of a former State Senator with name recognition, and an Assistant State's Attorney. I was starting mostly from scratch but ultimately won by a comfortable margin.

I wasn't always successful, however. Many years later, after leaving the legislature to re-engage in the community, I decided to challenge our popular 32-year State Senator. Despite out-fundraising and out-door-knocking and earning most of the

GEM 2

biggest endorsements (including the Washington Post, the environmental groups and the pro-choice group), I was around 300 votes short. Four years later, I was persuaded to try again. My opponent was my successor in the House – a 16-year incumbent. This time, I won.

Lesson #8: We're not all equal.
Those around us may be smarter, wealthier, more successful or better looking. In Scrabble, I know that there are hundreds of tournament players around the country who are ranked higher than me. But I study word lists, practice online, and compete often in order to improve. Similarly, we can work harder, invest wisely, and visit the gym more often in order to improve ourselves.

Lesson #9: There's no such thing as perfection.
A perfect Scrabble match is a fantasy for most of us. There's the "bingo" we didn't see, the phony word we didn't challenge and the mismanagement of our time clocks.

Each day, we are offered the chance to do the best we can. We may rarely get it exactly right, but, as I often tell my staff, "perfect is the enemy of the good." I'm picky, but sometimes we just need to get it done. Send the email, make the speech, and finish the home-repair project. Do the very best you can, but don't fret about an error.

Lesson #10: Have fun!
Scrabble is just a game. Those of us who compete take it pretty seriously. We refuse to play "Words with Friends," because it uses a different dictionary and, as such, could play tricks with our minds.

Years ago, a friend told me that the happiest people are those who live "in a place of gratitude." I am that person. I own a house (along with the bank) and a cute used car. I'm healthy and I get to do meaningful work with interesting and smart people. I also seize opportunities to volunteer and give back to my community and, as a result, have remarkably devoted and loving friends. I take very little for granted.

Life is not a game, as there is too much at stake. However, if you are willing to build on your assets, work hard, take risks, be mindful of your legacy and keep a healthy perspective, you're likely to be happy and successful – both in Scrabble and in life!

GEM 2

Gem 2 Essayist: **Cheryl Kagan**

Cheryl Kagan has served in the Maryland Senate since 2015, where her energy, dedication, and experience in all sectors–public, private, and nonprofit–make her an effective advocate for the residents of Gaithersburg and Rockville. She is a member of the Education, Health, and Environmental Affairs Committee; the Joint Audit Committee; the Joint Committee on Federal Relations; and chairs the Joint Committee on the Management of Public Funds.

A Montgomery County native and product of its public schools, Senator Kagan graduated from Vassar College with a degree in political science. She returned home with the aim of improving her community and later did graduate work in public policy at the University of Maryland. During her eight years in the Maryland House of Delegates (1995-2003), Kagan established a reputation as an independent-minded legislator with a strong voice for her constituents on issues such as fairness, public safety, fiscal priorities, and transportation.

After choosing not to seek reelection in 2002, she stayed involved in the community as the first-ever Executive Director of the Carl M. Freeman Foundation. Under her guidance, the Foundation contributed over $1,000,000 each year to deserving nonprofit organizations, primarily in the DC-metro area. In addition to grantmaking, the Foundation created capacity-building programs as well as a leadership institute in partnership with Montgomery College. Kagan later served as the Director of Community Engagement for BBYO, an international nonprofit organization promoting Jewish teen leadership and volunteerism for nearly a hundred years. There, she was responsible for community outreach, partnerships, fundraising, and media throughout the Mid-Atlantic. She has also taught State and local government at the college level. After falling just a few hundred votes short of winning a race for the Senate in 2010, Kagan was encouraged by legislative and community leaders, including retiring Senator Jennie Forehand, to run in 2014. She was victorious in one of the State's most closely watched races, defeating her successor in the House of Delegates, who had served for 16 years.

GEM 2

GEM 3

This I know for sure:
Black owned media must survive!

I am a second-generation owner of a Black-owned media company, which publishes *The Washington Informer* (The Informer), a community newspaper established in Washington, D.C. 53 years ago by my father, Dr. Calvin W. Rolark, Sr.

Dad was a community and civil rights activist, philanthropist, and journalist. He was born in 1927 and raised in Texarkana, Texas and had one older brother, Ross, Jr. He graduated from Prairie View A&M University in Texas in the mid-1940s following in the footsteps of his brother and mother who also graduated from college.

Upon graduation from Prairie View, he followed his brother by enlisting into the U.S. Army, and served two years as a paratrooper in the Korean War. He received an honorable discharge, and once again, he followed his brother and moved to Washington, D.C. He worked for the Army at the Pentagon and later became a life insurance agent for several black-owned insurance companies. He was a traveling insurance man and covered the area from D.C. to Tennessee.

In 1952, he married my mother, Vera McGlassom (Abbott), in D.C. and two years later I was born on December 26, 1954. Dad continued selling insurance for several years until local D.C. political and social justice issues caught his eye. Concerned about the lack of voting rights and the fight for self-determination, he became a community activist, participating in causes related to police brutality and the fight for D.C.'s home rule.

He first worked for a black-owned newspaper called *The New Observer*. It was located on Florida Avenue in what was referred to as the "Black Broadway" of D.C. Successful black-owned businesses such as the famous Ben's Chili Bowl, Scurlock Photography, The Howard Theatre, and many other thriving black-owned businesses were located there.

Around 1964, he decided to branch out on his own and start *The Washington Informer*. Divorced from my mother, he met Wilhelmina Jackson, a young lawyer, and married her in 1963. She gave my father the $500 he needed to start the newspaper that published its first issue on October 16, 1964. As a community newspaper, it reflected the issues of the day in the lives of black folk and the "hot button" issues, as well. At the time, two main issues dominated the news in the community: The need to fight racism and the need to establish home rule. What distinguished it from other forms of local black-owned media was its focus on important civic and social issues and not primarily on entertainment and sports. This is not to say that such topics weren't covered, rather, covering the full spectrum of black life was its aim.

Just as my dad was a community activist, so was my stepmother. She started the National Association of Black Women Attorneys and was active in other legal associations. She and my dad encouraged each other in their activism. When the opportunity came that allowed black people to run for the school board for the first time, my dad threw his hat in the ring. When he didn't win, he was done and proclaimed: "The hell with politics." His interest in becoming an elected official transferred to his wife.

My stepmother ran for a seat on the District's first elected city Council in in 1974 and lost. She was not dissuaded. She ran again and won and remained on the Council for 16 years representing Ward 8, which had been an all-white area but had transformed into an all-black area, and one of the poorest wards in the city. Separated by the Anacostia River, Ward 8 symbolized the realities of the white and black worlds in D.C.

My father and stepmother remained in Ward 8 until they died in 1994 and 2006, respectively. In 2006, I inherited the newspaper, which I have run since graduating from law school in 1979.

At that time, the Informer's circulation was about 15,000, although we often claimed a much larger number to attract advertising. Over 3,000 Washington area residents regularly subscribed to the newspaper and had it delivered to their homes. Newspapers were also circulated through business establishments including barber shops, restaurants, retail shops, churches, grocery stores, pharmacies and others— about 150 such locations in all.

As a tabloid-sized newspaper, then and still now, we averaged about 24 to 28 pages a week. Today, our average page count has doubled to 48 to 56 pages, and at times tripled, with positive news covering every aspect of African American life in D.C., from politics to sports, business, entertainment, and all matters of concern to the black community in Washington, D.C.

I started working at the newspaper at the age of nine, every summer, when the court-ordered joint custody allowed me to stay with my dad and stepmother. When I was in junior high school, I edited a column called "The Junior High Scene," and when I was

GEM 3

in high school, I wrote one called the "The High School Scene." Occasionally, I was assigned to cover stories, and at 14 and I traveled to Los Angeles, California to cover a D.C. girls track team at the national AAU Women's track meet where I interviewed Wilma Rudolph and Bill Cosby. Despite such exposure and opportunity, I wasn't sold on the newspaper business.

Understand, I grew up with friends who were indulged by their parents; they had everything. My dad wasn't into that and would never buy me a name brand anything. As a matter of fact, he discouraged me from buying into company names that did not support the Black community. I understood it better later when it was my turn to solicit advertising from companies that had no allegiance to its Black patrons.

It took a while for me to see the value in what my dad was doing. I enjoyed writing, but I was not a journalist. At the Informer, I reckoned I was just engaged in busy work and that when I came for the summer, my dad would say, "Give Denise something to do."

It was when I went to Hampton Institute, an historically black college in Virginia, that I had my first "a ha" moment. It came when I learned two days after the Vietnam War ended that it had ended. I realized that something was wrong with this picture. How is it that it took me two days to learn about it? I began to feel isolated and my desire to be back in the news capital of the world grew. So, I transferred to Howard University, in D.C., where the action was.

It was at Howard University that I had another "a ha moment," and it was the one that made me finally appreciate what a community newspaper means and its value to the community.

By the time I transferred into Howard, I had already become a little more civic minded, having been engaged in civic endeavors while at Hampton. I took political science courses as a precursor for law school, and later enrolled into Howard Law School hoping to pursue a career in International Communications Law. But this was before the Internet, cell phones, cable television and most of the technology we regularly use today. As a result, when I said I focus my legal studies in this area, everyone said, "What the heck is that?"

While in I was in law school, my dad turned over the newspaper to me. He probably thought I was ready because in undergraduate school, I wrote for Howard University's newspaper, *The Hilltop*, and later became the editor of *The Barrister*, the law school newspaper, while still going to the Informer office every day to publish our weekly newspaper. It's ironic though that I was learning while doing.

GEM 3

Even at this point, I still wasn't sold on the value proposition of a community newspaper and dedicating my life to it. The Dean of our law school wasn't sold on it either and didn't really care about *The Barrister*. All of that changed when Justice Thurgood Marshall was invited to dedicate the law school's newly built Moot Court Room in 1978.

Because I was the editor of the student newspaper, I couldn't also be in the role of interviewing the Justice, so I asked someone else to do it. When it was time to go to press, I asked the reporter for the article, he handed me a transcript. I asked, "Why did you do that?" And he explained, "because I am a court reporter and that's what we do when we report."

This was a problem. What to do? No one took notes from the ceremony and I had no story for an edition expected to be printed in two days. Given the situation, I decided to simply print Justice Marshall's speech verbatim. A novel idea!

It was a worldwide hit because Justice Marshall did not speak from a prepared speech. Everyone was calling the Dean asking for a copy of the newspaper. The Dean contacted me because he needed copies right away. As a result, Howard got a scoop "hot off the press!"

From then on, *The Barrister* became a respected news organ of the law school, starting with the Dean, who was also a corporate board member of Kodak. He funded the newspaper for a year and provided of rolls of film for the paper to use to continue capturing historical moments at the law school.

Now, I got it. I knew why newspapers were important: They were a source of power. Owning a newspaper was owning power.

I realized then that those who control the narrative, control the power.

"Ah hah", this is what my father had been doing all of those years, publishing good news for the benefit of Black people.

Now, *The Washington Informer* was in my hands. It has been in them ever since 1980. I have been at the helm longer than my dad.

When I think about the meaning and importance of a black-owned newspaper, I reflect on the words of Samuel E. Cornish, a minister and abolitionist, and John Brown Russwurm, an educator and abolitionist, who together started the first black newspaper in America, *The Freedom Journal* in Rochester, New York on March 16,

GEM 3

1927. They proclaimed in their first edition: "We wish to plead our own cause. Too long have others spoken for us."

These words still resonate today, as things haven't changed much or nearly enough. This was evident in the recent "March for Our Lives" in Washington, D.C. protest of school shootings. Young black students underscored that they who suffer gun violence all too often and reminded everyone that black lives matter too.

How black lives matter and how we contribute to society every day is what black community newspapers convey. They remind blacks to be proud and inform whites of our value.

Now, I too am clarified. I know why my dad started this newspaper and why I must continue with it, because it makes a difference and it matters. It records our history in our own words and reminds us of our humanity. It's important to leverage all media forms in the process, which is why today, our newspaper is just one of our vehicles; we are embracing and leveraging all forms of media to tell and record our stories for prosperity and for our survival.

Gem 3 Essayist: **Denise Rolark-Barnes**

Denise Rolark-Barnes is the publisher of *The Washington Informer*, the award-winning weekly newspaper serving the African American community in the Washington metropolitan area. She is a second-generation publisher, succeeding her father, Dr. Calvin W. Rolark, who founded the newspaper in 1964. In addition to her work at *The Washington Informer*, Rolark-Barnes maintains The Washington Informer Charities, a non-profit organization that promotes literacy and sponsors internship opportunities, writing competitions, and scholarships for students interested in pursuing careers in journalism. The Washington Informer Charities is also the official sponsor of the annual DC City-Wide Spelling Bee, and the Prince George's Spelling Bee in Maryland. Both are participants of the Scripps National Spelling Bee.

Rolark-Barnes is a dedicated community servant who has launched a variety of local initiatives serving underserved youths in the DC, Maryland and Virginia areas. She coordinated an effort to erect an anti-gang mural project in Southeast, D.C.; as well as a day of social and personal development for girls at Ballou Senior High School called "Girl Talk." She re-established the Martin Luther King Jr. Holiday Peace Walk and Parade in Ward 8, which is now in its 12th year. Most recently, Rolark-Barnes initiated the Annual Washington Informer African American Heritage Tour.

Rolark-Barnes is past chair of the National Newspaper Publishers Association – the Black Press of America. She serves on the boards of several local non-profit, community and municipal organizations, including the Washington Convention and Sports Authority (Events DC); the DC Martin Luther King Holiday Commission; National Newspaper Publishers Associationand Foundation; the Maryland, Delaware, DC Press Association; and the Anacostia Waterfront Initiative. She is also a member of Leadership Greater Washington. She is an inductee in the D.C. Hall of Fame, and a recipient of numerous awards including the Generous Heart Award presented by the Jack H. Olender Foundation. Rolark-Barnes is a graduate of Howard University where she received a BA degree in journalism and a JD degree from Howard University School of Law. She lives in the District of Columbia with her husband, Lafayette Barnes. They have two adult sons.

Contact: Denise Rolark-Barnes
The Washington Informer, 3117 MLK Jr. Ave., S.E. WDC 20032 (202) 561-4100
drbarnes@washingtoninformer.com and www.washingtoninformer.com

GEM 3

GEM 4

This I know for sure:
It's important to be politically active and to hold candidates to the highest standard of integrity.

I was born and raised in New York City, in the boroughs of Brooklyn and Queens, respectively, and I also went to law school there. As is the case for so many New Yorkers, I thought New York was the whole world, and could not have contemplated living anywhere else.

I got involved in politics after being inspired by former Presidents John F. Kennedy and Lyndon B. Johnson (before he destroyed himself by supporting the Vietnam War). I formed the Young Reform Democrats of Queens County, and participated in every election; I would carefully select candidates whom I felt would help people, and am glad to say that I usually selected well.

I believe that I learned the importance of charity and kindness from my father and the candidates he supported. My father was a great admirer of Franklin D. Roosevelt and the New Deal, knowing what it had offered for those most in need.

When in law school, I regularly organized forums in which students could hear from such people as Supreme Court Justice William O. Douglas and William Kunsler. Not all politicians are lawyers but many are, and I felt that having such speakers would help to educate my fellow students.

After moving to Washington, D.C. to take up a job with the federal government, my outlook on the world expanded and I finally realized that New York represented only a very small part of humanity, and an atypical part at that.

To further broaden my overall perspective, I became a "history buff" and read extensively about historical events and politics. I was particularly fascinated by and fixated on the Civil War and Abraham Lincoln. The more I read and learned, the more I viewed Lincoln as my ideal of what a politician and a man should be like. He was honest, prepared, and one of the most eloquent speakers and writers in American history.

When working as a lawyer for various trade associations later in my career, I kept the ideals of Lincoln in mind, and tried my best to lead others toward the correct path.

The people on the "right path," I know for sure, are kind and considerate toward other people; they are willing to help out and get involved, and are charitable and care about those who are less fortunate. There are many people who through no fault of their own – such as illness, circumstances of birth, or poverty – are not as fortunate as others. However, we need to remind ourselves that all people are created equal and have the same political and civil rights, as well as an equal obligation to be considerate and kind toward others and make a contribution, where possible.

In my personal life, the way I have contributed to society has been through participating in the political process at the local level. Although some people look down on politics, I view it as the most special form of service anyone can provide to others. Being politically active takes effort, and you will be criticized, but you must enter the field and make your political views known.

To be politically active, you do not have to be a candidate yourself, but you must be involved. One option is to help those you want to be elected, and to educate voters about candidates. There are many figures who followed this path: George Washington, John Adams, Alexander Hamilton, Lincoln, Theodore Roosevelt, Franklin D. Roosevelt, John F. Kennedy, and Barack Obama. I recommend reading about all of them to learn from their lives and examples about how to set your own goals. All these great leaders could have been more financially and personally successful, if they had been selfish and cared only for themselves. In the end, however, selfish people are forgotten, and those who care about others are remembered.

In my case, I have tried to help all candidates here in Montgomery County, not just the ones I plan to vote for; I try to be helpful to all of them, and recommend this approach to others. For example, I once wrote about some unusual policies affecting my homeowners' association, which happens to be a treasure trove of vote; however, I disseminated the paper to all candidates who were interested, regardless of their party affiliation. I also wrote a paper about basic communication techniques, because even the smartest candidates seem to forget them when in the heat of battle. Additionally, I try to provide information to as much of the electorate as I can reach, and especially to senior citizens.

If, in the course of your political activism, you become a candidate yourself, my advice is to always be honest, and to remain true to yourself. It is important to look for ways to leverage your position to help other people, and it's equally vital that you do not criticize others for personal reasons. Comment on their views, yes, but not on who they are.

GEM 4

33 Gems ✦ Wisdom for Living Pieces of Life's Puzzle

My advice to young people is that they should always vote for every office in every election. Find out what every candidate stands for, and vote for those you consider to be the best. Above all, vote in every election based on the knowledge that you have acquired through your research.

A final note: Just as important – if not more important – than the previous advice is to find true love. You may have to wait a long time, but don't give up. Seek to find a companion for life who will be loving, caring, helpful, funny, and who is on your intellectual level. Nothing could ever be more important in your life.

Gem 4 Essayist: **Paul Bessel**

Paul is a retired lawyer, having been a member of the Bar of the District of Columbia for 40 years and of the Bar of the State of Maryland for 8 years. He received his law degree from Columbia University Law School in 1972. He was born and raised in Brooklyn and Queens, New York, and attended Queens College and the Bronx High School of Science. He is active in his community of Montgomery County and Leisure World, and is Chairperson of the Montgomery County Charter Review Commission, and Treasurer of his community condo association at Leisure World. Previously, he was a member of the Ballot Issues Advisory Committee of the Montgomery County Democratic Central Committee in 2010 and 2012; Parliamentarian of the Montgomery County Democratic Central Committee (MCDCC); and served on the Executive Committee of the Democratic Club of Leisure World and Treasurer of the Democratic Club of District 19. He is a life-long Democratic, having campaigned for JFK and LBJ, founded the Young Democrats of Queens County (New York), and voted in every election, primary and general, since 1970.

He is Past President of the Maryland Association of Parliamentarians (MAP) and Past President of the Henry M. Robert III Unit of Parliamentarians, both groups within the National Association of Parliamentarians. In the past, he was General Counsel of a foundation that brought together high school age students from foreign countries, teaching leadership skills, teamwork, and the importance of tolerance and cooperation throughout the world.

GEM 4

Prior to that, he was in private law practice and held executive and legal positions with several organizations including national trade associations, and he was a Senior Attorney with the Civil Aeronautics Board, an agency of the United States government.

He is a member of Mensa and a Life Member of the Montgomery County Historical Society. He and his beloved wife serve each year as judges at National History Day, locally, statewide, and nationally, where high school and junior high school student compete with projects about historical subjects.

GEM 4

GEM 5

This I know for sure:
GOD "SHAPE-d" me to do what I am doing to help minority firms bridge the access-to-capital gap.

SHAPE-d is an acronym for **s**pirit, **h**eart, **a**bility, **p**ersonality and **e**xperiences. I was endowed with each of these critical assets in extraordinary ways at critical times.

I was born in 1947 in the deep South, in the low country of South Carolina. Historically, Black folk were situated very close to the water, so that they could not easily escape during times of slavery. This was even though the navigation of life on land was no less treacherous than that at sea.

My parents had figured life out; they were entrepreneurs just like their parents and grandparents before them. My father was not just any entrepreneur, he was a master bricklayer. He was known for using a type of bricks in his buildings called "Old English", which were much sought-after in combination with his highly honed skills as a craftsman. He knew he was in a seller's market and, although Black, he nevertheless was able to effectively negotiate the terms of his deals, making sure that his clients, White folk, would stick to those terms. If they did not, he would get half way through a building project and walk away from it until the client agreed to his terms.

My father was segregated but not disenfranchised. He was enfranchised through his vocational skills and business cunning, as well as through the help of an important network, a secret society of Black Masons. I obtained only glimpses into just how important this network was.

I remember that, on Sundays, dad used to drive us around in a car to nowhere because, at the time, we were not allowed to go in anywhere. So, we packed a picnic lunch and pulled over on the side of the road as our outing for the day. Once, we got a flat tire on the way back home and my dad said, "don't worry, check this out." He started making hand signs and gestures – the next thing we knew, a line of cars was pulling over to help us. The hand signs and gestures were codes used by the Black Masons.

To this day I do not know what the society is all about and my father never revealed any information about it. All I knew was that it was powerful and that everyone in it had a duty and obligation to help each other out. My dad promised that when I got to the "anteroom" the secret would be revealed to me but, sadly, I never got there. Wherever that was and whatever that meant, none of the secrets of the Black Masons were ever revealed to me. One thing I knew, though, was that having skills and a network were pieces of the puzzle of economic empowerment and of maintaining dignity as Black males.

I also learned another important lesson from my mother, which was and is the importance of spirituality. If having money is important, the meaning of its importance is to be found in one's spirituality. So, before the usual Sunday rides to nowhere, we went to church, to one of those serious non-denominational churches that thrived in the deep South. The preachers there could really preach; later, I was to realize that I had learned public speaking from them.

Though it was a tough environment to grow up in, I thrived. It was sad when my parents broke up and my four siblings and I had to move up north to Long Island, New York. I was fifteen at the time and joined a public school. Here, I was taught alongside White students for the first time. Those Black teachers in the south had taught me well, and I was on par with my new classmates.

Life moved at a faster speed in New York: they don't call it a "New York minute" for nothing. Soon enough I was smoking weed, partying, and having a good time. Naturally, coming from a family of entrepreneurs, it dawned on me that I shouldn't just smoke weed: I should sell it.

By the time I entered college at Morgan State University in Baltimore, Maryland, I was proficient at selling weed. One day, while I was bagging it up in the basement, my mom came in and saw me and was horrified. She told me that one day I would go to jail. Sure enough, her warning came to pass. I was caught up in a sting operation and was arrested and sent to jail. I was incarcerated for over two years. My wife was eight months pregnant and stranded, and my college education was interrupted in my junior year.

Now life's lessons started pouring in, fast and furious. I was lucky, however: at every turn, there were angels watching over me. As I reflect on my life, there were eight major times, I experienced a divine intervention that shaped my life.

Divine intervention #1: "Tree Stump", my cell mate (named for his physique) was a guiding angel. The first day I entered the cell, he said "Would you like a cigarette?" Though I didn't smoke, I said yes and smoked it. Then he asked me a second time and a third; each time I accepted and smoked the cigarette. After the third time, he said: "Let me to tell how to survive in this joint. You don't belong here, so this is what you must do to survive: One, never accept any gifts from anyone. Two, don't gamble, and three, don't go anywhere near the 'punk boys'". I followed his advice.

GEM 5

Divine intervention #2: I was sent to a processing center, which would determine to which jail I would be sent. Surprisingly, the processor (who was a White male) had graduated from the presumed all-Black Morgan State University. Because of this connection, he was instrumental in sending me to a minimum-security prison.

Divine intervention #3: Johnny protected me. I used to play ball in the prison yard and was very friendly with everyone. So, when I noticed that Johnny was all by himself and no-one ever talked to him, I went over to him and introduced myself, and we talked. The other fellas in the yard thought I was crazy. They said, "Do you know who Johnny is?" He had been saved from the electric chair twice and had killed someone for bumping into him who hadn't said "excuse me". So, I told Johnny what they said about him and he confirmed that it was true. He explained that he wanted them to think that he was crazy so that they'd leave him alone. Johnny, like me, was an avid reader, and we bonded on that level. Because people saw me talking to him, no one ever bothered me.

Divine intervention #4: I learned many valuable and fundamental lessons in prison, chief among which was understanding the importance of keeping my wits about me always. "Eyes and ears wide open and mouth shut." To this day, when I walk in a room I scan and process it in an instant: where are the doors? Where are the exits? What types of people are in the room? More importantly, in human interactions, I am 100 percent present and engaged, and I always look into the eyes of those with whom I'm interacting, which allows me to make a judgement about them.

Divine intervention #5: After I was released from prison, Morgan State accepted me back. This time, I took a serious approach to my study, making it onto the Dean's List. Some of the angels who were looking out for me there gave me a job upon graduation to help me out, as by then I had a family and two kids. I then found out that Baltimore City had a special program, whereby if any of it minority residents were accepted into one of the top ten MBA programs in the U.S., the city would help to pay for their study.

So, I applied to Columbia. I went there for a visit and, when I was in the lobby, a person yelled out "Hey, Stan!" He was a former classmate from Morgan State who would then intervene on my behalf to ensure my acceptance into the program at Columbia. I was all set to attend Colombia when, thirty days before, a letter arrived at my house introducing me to Carnegie Mellon University (CMU) in Pittsburgh. I had never heard of CMU; however, I decided to visit it.

Divine intervention # 6: I took a bus to Pittsburgh to visit CMU. As soon as I saw the campus, its quad reminded me of Morgan State. A feeling came over me and I knew

GEM 5

I was supposed to go there. When I told my wife, she was shocked but agreed, and off we went.

As soon as we got to Pittsburgh, I started searching around for a program in nutrition that my wife could attend. Surprisingly, none of the larger universities in Pittsburgh had a nutrition program. However, I found a smaller women's college, Seton Hill College, that did. It was located 30 miles outside of Pittsburgh. I took a bus there and went directly to the President's office. It was quite shocking to see a Black man simply show up at the President's office of this all-White school. The receptionist asked if I had an appointment: I did not. To cut a long story short, against all odds the President agreed to see me. Incredibly, after chastising me for daring to show up at her office, when she learned that I was trying to help my wife, she arranged for full tuition for my wife on the spot.

So, we had two kids in tow, both my wife and I in school, and my wife had to drive 60 miles a day. Somehow, we made it work.

Divine intervention #7: In the School of Public Policy at Carnegie-Mellon there was a one-year-long "Systems Synthesis" project-based course. The project had to involve an important public policy issue, so I rallied a few of my friends to lobby for us to work on a minority business.

No-one had ever done such a project. We got the green light and started working with Pittsburgh's small business administration (SBA) office and with other agencies that focused on minority businesses. The critical thing I learned is that minority firms didn't have access to capital. From then on, I knew what my life's mission would be: bridging the capital gap for minority firms.

Divine intervention #8: "Show me the money!" Literally. I knew that I needed to gain an understanding of banking as my next move after graduation. I was interviewed by Equitable Bank and, again, I was lucky to encounter a former classmate from Morgan State. He was instrumental in escalating my case for review, which ultimately went all the way to the Chairman's desk.

The question was: should we hire an "ex-con" to work in banking? The Chairman contacted Ray Haysbert, who had been a professor at Morgan State and who was a member of the Board of Directors of the bank and asked him if he knew me. He vouched for me and I got the job. While employed at Equitable, I learned how credit decisions were made and was then ready to move on.

GEM 5

At this point, I had wings. I joined a community development organization that lent funds to minority-owned firms. Soon after I got there, and after being mentored by its director, the director departed, and I took his place. The first thing I did was reach back to someone with whom I had worked with at Equitable, a woman who was more knowledgeable about banking than me.

Together, we created a master plan and a strategy with which to bridge the capital gap to provide more and multidimensional funding for minority firms.

Now, I had to put in motion all that had "**SHAPE-d**" me.

You must understand, there is a reason why minority firms and Black-owned firms were disenfranchised: it was orchestrated that way. Our community-funding organization was state-owned. We had state funds, but we also wanted federal and private funds. So, we approached the United States' SBA. It cited regulations that required federal-matching funds to come from the private sector. At that time, we didn't have private funds. However, we developed a strategy that ultimately worked for us.

Making the law work for us

Laws are words, and words can change. I used all the arrows in my "**SHAPE-d**" quiver and got to work. The key was to mobilize the federal legislative apparatus; we appealed to the minority members of Congress, asking them to change the definition of the term "private funds". We prevailed and were able to access SBA funds, which we then injected into our small-business investment company (SBIC). This meant that we could no longer be state employees and would have to give up our job security. We had to privatize and leave our government positions, which we did. As it turned out, we chose wisely, eventually becoming what we are today: The Meridian Management Group (MMG).

It's a war, not a single battle

For the next 22 years, and every step of the way, we have had to mobilize, strategize, and understand how to pull government levers at both state and federal levels. We have reinterpreted and changed the legal framework in our fight to support minority firms.

Arguably, our greatest win was getting a percentage of the gaming revenue in our state, to set aside in a fund whose purpose was to help small, minority and women-owned businesses. This seemingly small amount of 1.5 percent of gaming proceeds has thus far yielded over $50 million for minority firms over the past four years.

GEM 5

The battlefield is also inside of us

After 22 years of lending and investing hundreds of millions of dollars to entrepreneurs, I have learned one thing: entrepreneurial endeavors will succeed or fail depending on the quality of the entrepreneur. It's not the industry, the product, or the service that will determine the success of a venture; it's the quality of the entrepreneur and what has **SHAPE-d** him or her.

I am an advocate and, while people talk about the importance of both advocacy and networking, they need to more deeply understand both the power and limitations of this position. To create wealth, we need both access to capital and quality entrepreneurs.

Finally, through all the trials and tribulations in my life, God has always been in the mix. As such, I rely implicitly on God's word, particularly Psalm 27(14): "Don't be impatient, wait for the Lord and he will come and save you, but while waiting, be bold, strong, and courageous."

Yes: wait, and he will help you.

GEM 5

Gem 5 Essayist: **Stanley Tucker**

Stanley W. Tucker has more than 30 years of diversified business experience with a strong emphasis on lending, venture capital investing and the development of socially or economically disadvantaged small businesses. Mr. Tucker is President, Chief Executive Officer and co-founder of Meridian Management Company, Inc (MMG). The firm manages four comprehensive program funds: the Maryland Small Business Development Financing Authority (MSBDFA); Maryland Casino Business Investment Fund (MCBIF); Community Development Ventures, Inc. (CDV); and MMG Ventures, LP (MMGV) which provides its clients with every opportunity a company needs to grow and succeed. Mr. Tucker also serves as the Managing Partner of MMG Ventures, LP and President of Community Development Ventures, Inc. Prior to forming Meridian Management Group, he was the Executive Director of the Maryland Small Business Development Financing Authority (MSBDFA), 1981 to 1995. MSBDFA is a self-sufficient state agency that assists socially or economically disadvantaged businesses. Combined, MMG managed programs have provided over $232 million financing to small, minority, and women owned businesses located in Maryland.

Mr. Tucker provides the vision for the overall organization. He is involved in the marketing strategy; initiating, structuring, syndicating and monitoring of investments, as well as review of financial reports and financial plans for MMG and its family of funds, and is materially involved in the analysis, review and approval of investment proposals and in monitoring the portfolio. Mr. Tucker was Vice President of the Park Heights Development Corporation (PHDC), a community-based economic development corporation located in one of Baltimore's highest crime and unemployment areas from 1980 to 1981. At PHDC, he raised $1.2 million for the first stage development of a community industrial park and garnered additional funding for a community business loan fund, which he oversaw. Prior to joining PHDC, he was a credit analyst for Equitable Trust Company of Baltimore. Mr. Tucker's present and past civic responsibilities include: Chairman of the Golden Bears Association, Inc. and the National Association of Investment Companies; President's Roundtable, Baltimore Youth Alliance, the MD/DC Minority Supplier Development Council; Warner Press; H. John Heinz, III School (Carnegie-Mellon University); Sojourner-Douglas College; and the Morgan State University Foundation. Mr. Tucker received his bachelor's degree from Morgan State University and Master's degree from Carnegie-Mellon University's Heinz School.

GEM 5

GEM 6
This I know for sure:
God is real and His word is true.

I grew up in Washington, D.C., originally in the Michigan Park area then in Crestwood, living in a home with hard-working parents. We were ordinary middle-class people: I went to a private elementary, a public junior high, then attended a Catholic high school even though I wasn't Catholic. In the process, I met and interacted with people of all types and backgrounds. My parents weren't terribly religious people and were members of separate churches; if it was up to me, I wouldn't have attended either church. When my mother stopped making me go, I stopped going. I did believe in God, however, and religion was always respected in the family. A photo of the Last Supper of Jesus Christ hung in my grandmother's house as a reminder.

Both of my parents were dedicated to the Black community and did all they could to help people, as they believed in giving back. My father was the owner and president of a black-owned community bank in Washington, D.C., as was his father before him. He and many others probably assumed I would be president of the bank one day and it eventually turned out that way. My father was quiet around the house and was, in general, a man of few words who didn't seem terribly comfortable addressing personal and emotional situations or issues. In the business environment, he was different, however. By contrast, my mother was a disciplinarian and ran the business of the house; she confronted issues in a direct, in-your-face, but mostly loving way.

My mother was a junior high-school music teacher in the D.C. public school system, eventually retiring after 30 years of service. Her father was a struggling musician who dedicated his life to chasing his dream of "making it" in music as an opera singer. He had a great voice, but the discrimination at that time meant that a fair-skinned black person such as he wasn't offered the opportunity to rise as an opera singer in the United States. As a result, he ran away to Germany after my mother and her sisters were grown.

My mother was feisty, to say the least, and I believe that she had sour feelings about her father leaving the family to go to his "Hollywood" in an aim to be discovered. However, music was important to her too; each night I fell asleep listening to her practice the piano and preparing for the lessons she would impart to her students. Eventually, music would become my greatest love as well.

Music was also my cousin's greatest love; I recall that we would sing along to records

GEM 6

and have our own mini "concerts" when we spent weekends together. He was four years older than me and I loved the ground he walked on. He always put music bands together and played gigs around the city. By the age of 14, I became his little "road manager", which was a fancy way of saying that I'd find friends to attend his gigs and transport the equipment to them, "setting up" for ten bucks. He was an excellent songwriter and, by the time I was 16, he started recording songs. I was present in the recording studio and watched him and others record demo tapes. The experience inspired my desire to become a drummer, but mom wasn't having it.

With my dreams of becoming a drummer put on ice, I entered Rutgers University, undecided on a major. While at university, I worked at our bank during the summers. I learned a lot there. What made the biggest impression on me was the realization that, through banking, I could help people while making money at the same time. Once I came to this realization, my path to becoming a banker was laid.

As one might imagine, however, while on the winding road to becoming a banker I was exposed to many influences that also made an impression on me. Having gone to public school and having regularly hung out with older musicians exposed me to, shall we say, some of the darker pleasures of life. As a result, I got into quite a bit of mischief myself.

By the time I was 24, I knew things had to change in my life and I was moved to give my life over to Jesus. As it turned out, I had changed courses just in time. Just before I made this decision, I met a woman while we were serving jury duty. I had nearly been arrested myself just a few weeks earlier during a run-in with an off-duty detective. I could hear my mother saying, "Son, watch yourself, if you get into trouble it could ruin your chances of becoming the president of the bank one day." Wouldn't you know, at the courthouse during jury duty, I saw the same detective who almost arrested me. Luckily, he didn't see me, and I was able to avoid him.

Coincidence? I don't think so. God puts or allows us to be in situations when He is trying to get our attention. I saw that detective three times, but each time he didn't see me. In my interpretation, it was God's love for me that finally encouraged me to stay away from danger and to follow Him instead.

A few years later, I was renting a house with two other friends, both of whom attended the same church that I had begun to attend. One of my roommates was a high-school friend who was part of the "running hard" club I was in years earlier. He had developed the mental illness called manic depression disorder, a few years earlier. He functioned well as long as he stuck to his treatment program, but when he didn't he suffered manic episodes that could be quite extreme, including threatening us with violence.

GEM 6

My other roommate and I prayed quite a bit in those days, and for good reason. One manic episode to which we were exposed involved a rifle and a caged bird being cooked, during which time our manic roommate wouldn't allow us to leave the house. Cell phones weren't in common use back then, so we had to rely on our wits to escape. After several hours, we did escape from the house and headed to a friend's house to call the police. This too exposed us to danger. Police and a Black man with a gun did not mix, so I was afraid for our roommate's life during the encounter with the police. After much prayer, and the closing-off of the neighborhood streets by police, my friend was taken to the hospital, unharmed. We were then mindful of God's words: "He will give His angels charge over me, to keep me in all His ways."

Ten years later, now president of the bank, I backslid into some bad habits (mostly drinking) after experiencing several years' worth of fierce battles with banking regulators. Bank regulators have extremely broad powers and frequently target executives when things don't go so well. They didn't understand minority banks, didn't choose to, and had the full resources and power of the federal government to use against us if they chose to do so.

No excuses here though. I held up well professionally, but not personally. The funny thing about God's word, however, is that it says that, "after we clean our house and allow or return to old bad habits, we will be worse off than we were before" (Matthew 12:43-45). That was what came to pass in my case.

After several instances of God's grace in action, such as waving me through police checkpoints where, in basketball parlance, I might have "blown a 'triple-double'", God allowed the prodigal son to come home. I know for sure that His unconditional love abounds through His forgiveness, even though it still rains on "the just and unjust."

Last year, my best friend of 38 years committed suicide, seemingly out of nowhere. God says that He "will never give us more than we can handle" but that was a close one which, for me, tested those words. After counseling, I'm pretty sure I will make it through; I have realized that there are even worse tragedies that others have had to endure.

In some ways, I am thankful for what He has allowed me to go through. I know for sure that He is always with us, even though we think we are doing wonderful things on our own or when we are faced with adversity. His word says that "without Him, we can do nothing", but it's important to recognize that it doesn't say we are nothing.

Through thick and thin, I have learned that God is present everywhere, at all times. If I make my bed in hell, His word says that "He is with me." We are all imperfect and the

GEM 6

world is both puzzling and challenging, but we all have access to the love of God; while this may sometimes exceed our comprehension, it is within our grasp. At least, that's what I know.

✦ ✦ ✦

Gem 6 Essayist: **Doyle Mitchell**

B. Doyle Mitchell Jr. is CEO of Industrial Bank, the only minority-owned community bank in the Washington Metropolitan area and the sixth largest African-American owned institution in the country. Industrial Bank was founded in August 1934 to serve black people that were not served by other institutions due to discrimination. Today, the Bank serves everyone who is not well served by other institutions.

Mr. Mitchell was raised in the Washington banking community that his father and grandfather helped create. He worked summers at the Bank beginning at age 16 and worked from the ground up. He received his bachelor's in economics from Rutgers University, graduated from the American Institute of Banking and attended the Marymount University's graduate school of business. He succeeded his father as president in 1993.

Under Mr. Mitchell's leadership, Industrial Bank expanded into Prince George's County, Maryland in 1994, even before the Interstate Banking Bill was passed. Treasury Secretary, Lloyd Bentsen recognized him as a pioneer in the banking industry during the signing of the Bill by President Clinton.

Mr. Mitchell is a member of the U.S. Black Chambers, Inc. President's Circle, the Archbishop Carroll High School President's Council, board member of the Anacostia Business Improvement District, Venture Philanthropy Partners, member of the Independent Community Bankers of America's Regulatory Safety and Soundness Committee and the New Sewell Music Conservatory.

Mr. Mitchell (or the Bank) has received the Lifetime Legacy Award from the DC Chamber of Commerce, the Minority Business Leaders Award from the Washington Business Journal, the Torch Award from the National Newspaper Publishers Association Foundation, the Greater Prince George's Business Roundtable Chairman's Award, the Human Servant Award from Training Grounds DC, the Business Leader of the Year from the Prince George's Chamber of Commerce and countless others.

Mr. Mitchell is the immediate Past-Chairman of the National Bankers' Association and his vision is to make a difference in people's lives and grow the minority banking industry.

GEM 6

GEM 7

This I know for sure:

God has given me the ability to discern the good and bad in life and to harness its lessons to turn every obstacle into a stepping stone for reaching higher goals in my business and life.

I am the President and owner of Zavda Technologies, LLC ("Zavda") an Information Technology (IT) company. My company holds prime contracts with the Department of Defense (DoD) to provide state-of-the-art IT, intelligence, and cyber security services. To say I have come a long way is an understatement.

The distance I have come to arrive at this destination is as far as from the earth to the moon, and traveling the journey was just as perilous.

My journey began when I was born in 1974 in a small city in northeast Texas called Longview, but I was raised in an even smaller town named Carthage. Despite its auspicious name, Carthage was far from any semblance of greatness and the circumstances of my birth were far from desirable. My biological father was very violent. He rolled over in the bed and killed their first child, and when my mother was seven months pregnant with me, he pushed her off a porch nearly ending her pregnancy. That was the final violent incident that gave her the strength to finally leave him.

Each event surrounding my life growing up, and as an adult, always had two sides, the Yin and the Yang, the good and the bad. The good news of the story surrounding my birth is that while still pregnant with me, my mother found and married her mate for life, a good man, to whom she is still married and who has been a great father to me.

My parents were flat out poor and both barely had an opportunity to attend high school. Mom worked in a chicken factory and dad was a construction worker. Making ends meet was difficult but we had the leftover chicken from the local factory to supplement our diet, along with the vegetables and hogs we grew and raised on our 17 acres of land.

Both of my parents understood the value of education and pushed me forward in every way they could. However, neither was able to help me with my homework in my adolescent years. There were times when I felt really bad in comparing myself to the other students who knew more than me.

GEM 7

Academically, I was on my own but I never lacked the advocacy and emotional support of my parents while in school. When things got tough for me in school and I didn't know how I was going to make it, my mom went to the school to plead with the teachers in person for them to give me a fair chance, one that was equivalent to that being given to the white students.

When one of the teachers in elementary school grabbed me by my neck and left a bruise, that was the final straw! My parents took the extraordinary step of moving us out of Carthage to Fort Worth, Texas, followed by Abilene, Texas in search of a better environment. It was short-lived, however, as my dad wanted to return to Carthage to be near his family. In the short time I was in Abilene, I excelled in school like never before because the teachers treated me as just a student; not as a black student who was considered to be inferior.

When we returned to Carthage it was with the understanding that it was "make it or break it" time. Every one of us had to step up and share the load in order to propel the family forward. As the oldest, my job was to take care of the kids and just about everything else in the house while my parents worked day and night, literally. Mom decided to become a cosmetologist and was in school during the day and apprenticed in the evening. She had to quit her job at the chicken factory and my dad had to work hard to make up for the lost income. Sometimes, his construction jobs took him away for weeks at a time.

Upon completing her cosmetology course and apprenticeship and obtaining her license, my mom opened her own barber shop. For me, nothing changed: I was still in charge of the household and of myself. On the latter front, I had a breakthrough in my school work and began to sail through. In fact, I did so well that I entered college while simultaneously completing high school. Organization was the key. Essentially being the defacto "head of the household" since I was nine years old, I wasn't playing—literally. My life was about taking care of the kids, doing my school work, and as a family, going to church—dad was a deacon and a lay preacher as well. Church played a prominent role in shaping my value system and my commitment to "being a good girl."

When I graduated from high school, I received scholarships to attend many universities but even with full scholarships, I still needed some money but we had none. Instead of going directly to college, I decided to go into the military and looked for the best benefit package that would enable me to continue college during my service. The Air Force offered the best benefits, so that's the route I took.

GEM 7

Boy, being in the military was an eye-opening experience! I had never heard curse words spoken so openly, nor had I ever experienced someone constantly yelling at me. One thing was familiar, how things were regimented and organized. Just as the military ran on organization, so did I. Having run my parent's household in a military fashion from the time I was a child, the military felt familiar and I embraced its systems, discipline, and organization and excelled as a result.

The good news of this chapter of my story is that I adapted well to military service and was rewarded with regular promotions. The bad news is that I met a bad man who was a Dr. Jekyll and Mr. Hyde. As is usually the case in such situations, the relationship started out so nicely and he was so charming, as charming as I was naive; he insisted on us getting married and because of my "goody two shoes" predilection, I consented. It was all bad, and I barely made it out of it with my life, to make a long story short.

The next chapter of my life was good. I met and married my current husband. He was in the military too and we were stationed in some of the same places. He was a good man from the start, and has remained that way all the way through our 22 years of marriage to date. All was going along smoothly until I accepted an assignment to go to the desert in Saudi Arabia. While there, I contracted the mysterious "Gulf War Syndrome." Ever since, I have been sick off and on and have been afflicted with debilitating migraines, severe allergies, gastrointestinal illnesses, and other syndrome related ailments. As a result, I required medical waivers for my disabilities to be able to continue to serve in the Air Force. Despite this, I continued to excel in my military career.

When I returned from the Gulf, I was selected to support the White House Communications Agency (WHCA) and also won an Air Force Reserve Officer Training Corps (AFROTC) competition for extraordinary enlisted members in the United States Air Force (USAF). I received a scholarship to attend any university in the United States. Up to that point, although I had stayed in school, the highest degree I was able to attain was that of an Associate's Degree, due to my constant military reassignments. Despite having been blessed with so many promising opportunities, in the end, because my husband's next assignment was at Andrews Air Force Base (AFB), I chose to attend University of Maryland.

Having received an honorable discharge upon returning to the U.S., I enrolled in Officer Cadet Training at University of Maryland. By doing so, I was able to continue my college studies, live on the base, and have access to the commissary. One thing

GEM 7

I didn't have, however, was a salary. My husband was still in the service and without two incomes we were poor. It was hard, but that didn't stop me from obtaining my undergraduate degree in Computer Science, Master's in Information Technology, and a Ph.D. in Management. Of course, in keeping with the arc of my life, there were many twists and turns along this path as well, including the complications I experienced during my first pregnancy with my oldest child. Due to the "Gulf War Syndrome" I had contracted, the pregnancy was extremely difficult. Fortunately, my son and I survived and I was able to complete my sophomore and junior years of college while my husband was deployed overseas. Later, as I was obtaining my Master's Degree, I got pregnant with our second child and because the impact of the syndrome had worsened, the pregnancy almost killed me.

In the ups and downs of my life, the good news is that I have overcome all obstacles and have been strengthened in so doing. Each one of my obstacles was a stepping stone that I used to climb up to the next rung in the ladder of my success in business and life. When I encounter challenges in my business, I put on my "hard hat" and start plowing through it. This winning attitude, together with the state-of-the-art knowledge, the skills that our staff possess, and being able to draw on lessons learned in the military and throughout life, are among the ingredients that have made Zavda Technologies a success. As we continue to grow, we will continue to convert every obstacle we encounter into a stepping stone to build on our foundation and to move up higher.

As I reflect on my life, a few common themes come into sharp focus. One is that no matter what trials I have endured in life... discrimination, racism, rejection, inadequacies, verbal and physical abuse, death of loved ones, near death experiences, I always made the choice not to be a victim but rather to use these things to help me become a better and stronger person. I have also realized that my faith and upbringing have empowered me to overcome setbacks, and that the faith of my parents helped them overcome theirs as well. Last but not least, I know that everything in life happens for a reason and that I wouldn't be where I am today without my experiences. I view every day that I am alive as a blessing and as an opportunity for greatness.

Today, I am a successful owner, President, CEO and leader of Zavda Technologies, LLC, a security cleared, SBA 8(a) graduate and Small Disadvantaged Business (SDB) certified, Service Disabled Veteran and Economically Disadvantaged Woman Owned Small Business, which is privately owned, founded in 2006. Zavda is a multimillion dollar thriving business in the federal contracting arena. Due to my technical capabilities and in part to my charismatic personality and positive outlook on life, I have been able to diversify and expand my firm's portfolio of services from IT services to subject matter expertise in such areas as: cyber intel and linguistic analysis; network management; software development; systems engineering; and training. Additionally, by drawing on my life experiences, I have been able to successfully delegate tasks, roles, and responsibilities to other leaders within Zavda and have been instrumental in boosting Zavda's portfolio of contracts to more than 31 awarded long-term contracts.

From a little backwater town, I have moved as far away from it as the moon and I know for sure that my journey, even on the rough roads, was blessed by God. My husband and I are both the leaders and the glue for our respective families and just as we have been a blessing to them, God has blessed us in return. With our two children, ages 19 and 16, and with our growing businesses, "the best is yet to come," as my father reminds me all the time.

✦ ✦ ✦

Gem 7 Essayist: **Stacy Trammell, Ph.D.**

Dr. Trammell founded Zavda Technologies in June 2006 because she had a vision of what an IT Solutions company should look like from both the customer and the employee's perspective. Zavda has a loyal customer base and a team of devoted and hardworking employees who cannot imagine working elsewhere.

Dr. Stacy Trammell received her Doctorate of Management degree from the University of Maryland University College (UMUC) on May 16, 2009. Her research includes the identification of "The Best Practices of Small IT Services Providers in the Federal Arena", (ProQuest UMI Dissertation Publishing). She also has a Master's of Science degree in Information Technology Management from UMUC, and a Bachelor's of Science degree in Computer Science from the University of Maryland, among other degrees and certifications. In addition to her academic accomplishments, Dr. Trammell is a Service-Disabled Veteran of the United States Air Force and has served in various private and public agencies for more than 20 years.

GEM 7

Dr. Trammell's success is due in large part to a combination of her hands-on experience, academic preparation, and attitude. Dr. Trammell is a charismatic and passionate leader, and is at her core, someone who seeks to serve others —whether an employee, a business partner, or a government agency; in short, she strives to make a positive contribution to her community and to the world. Her positive attitude is contagious and she inspires and empowers both her employees and her colleagues. The attitudes of employees and customers are perhaps the best barometers of a leader's effectiveness, and it's rare when one manages to strike the perfect balance, as Dr. Trammell has. Zavda employees and customers alike have referred to Dr. Stacy Trammell as the kind of leader who the "Women Who Mean Business" and "Executive Business Leader" awards were created to honor. Not surprisingly, Dr. Trammell is the recipient of these and many others awards.

GEM 7

GEM 8

This I know for sure:
Success, growth, and meaning in life come from human connections that one must always cultivate.

As an only child, I often felt alone and adrift. My parents, depression children, from southern Illinois, lived in fear and isolation at all times. They feared the return of economic hard times; they feared big cities and Big Government, and they feared people who did not look like them, white, rural, and ill-educated. To a child, these fears came as received wisdom rather than as prejudice or a limited worldview. Like all parents, they thought they understood the world and they set out to educate me through language and behavior. Unfortunately, their language reflected bigotry and my behavior was sometimes subject to harsh punishment or frequent belittling. My mother came not to trust the man she married, so I learned that men were no good and, and of course, I was a little man. My father thought to be a man required independence and complete self-absorption. Both came from the bottom of a liquor bottle. As a child, I just wanted to play, to have friends, and to enjoy people around me. We moved from Illinois to Missouri to Louisiana to California to Texas all before I turned eight years old. I thought I could simply not make friends because my mother called me by a girl's name, Shelly.

Growing up in Odessa, in deep West Texas, I learned that most of the people in that city, the fastest growing town in America in the 1950s, came from somewhere else and most, but not all, shared my parents' attitudes and fears. The town was rabidly conservative, but it was diverse. I met Jewish people, Hispanic people, kids from big cities, and I met and interacted with African-Americans who worked at my dad's car wash. I now consider it fortunate that I began working at the car wash at eight years old (to learn the value of a dollar, you understand). At the car wash, the black folks I met became an alternative universe to the other one around me. They were smart, funny, good-hearted, and most of all, human in their good and bad traits. I simply could not make generalizations about them like the ones I often heard from my parents and friends. Civil rights to me became human rights. I was 10 at the time.

Odessa's then excellent schools afforded opportunities to learn formally and to play sports. The latter was no small matter since Texas is famous for football and the teams from Odessa then and in the immediate future were among the greatest in the nation.

GEM 8

My high school, Odessa Permian, became a symbol of sports' obsession in America through a book, a movie, and a TV show, "Friday Night Lights." I decided in the fifth grade to become a football player to overcome my fears and to prove myself worthy as a man. The man I wanted to impress most, my father, chose not to come to my games, but other connections I made with teammates and coaches helped me learn to set goals, work hard, and perform within a group to achieve excellence. My last coach also saw a spark of intelligence in me, so he gave me the "Oxford History of the English Language" as a graduation gift. I also received the "Outstanding Senior Man Award" as I graduated high school, but it made little difference to me then because just a year before one of my most important human connections, my first cousin, Betty Williams, was murdered. I was in a fog for more than a year after that.

Betty was a year older than I. She shared my Southern Illinois roots and the influences of a family rooted in evangelicalism, rural values, and male dominance. Betty and I did not grow up together, but she moved to Odessa at 12 when I was 11. She immediately became by most important connection. She was fast becoming an actor, an irrepressible personality, and a rebel. Our long talks about family, politics, race, relationships, and most of dreams about escaping Odessa helped me understand the world and myself in it. She was my mentor. She was also an emerging Hippie but, in her senior year, she was killed. I have written the details of all this in a book, but in the trial of the boy who killed her, she was painted as an evil temptress and he was cast as the victim. Nothing has ever rocked my world as much as her loss and that trial.

Directly as a result of that event I also met a girl who became my wife to this day. At ages 19 and 18 we married in part to save each other and to create a life based on love and equality rather than fear and ignorance. We paid our own ways through college, got scholarships for me to train as an educator, and worked together to get her through college 14 years later. She became a civil servant in the Social Security Administration. Our two children were never taught fear and hatred.

These events and lessons made me into a professor. I wanted to help young people not only learn from lectures and books but to become part of something bigger whether it was a college, a Model UN Team, a Leadership Program or global citizenship. I wanted to be there for them as an educator, a mentor, and a window to a possible future. I took them to Russia, China, New York, Germany, and Washington, D.C. When they lost their parents' favor for being gay, switching majors, or choosing the wrong political party, I was there to listen. I served in the government four times but always returned to college teaching to share my insights with students. Later, I began writing

GEM 8

a series of books to let others know that if they wish to base their lives on love and understanding, they are not in fact alone.

✦ ✦ ✦

Gem 8 Essayist: **Shelton "Shelley" Williams**

Shelton Williams is Founder and President of the Osgood Center for International Studies. He holds a M.A. and Ph.D. degrees from the Johns Hopkins University School of Advanced International Studies and is a Professor Emeritus of Political Science at Austin College. He has worked in the U.S. Government in the U.S. Trade Representative's Office, the Nuclear Regulatory Commission, the U.S. Department of State, and the Arms Control and Disarmament Agency. He has previously written extensively on the subject of nuclear proliferation and since 2004, has written mostly about crime and U.S. society. His latest novel is a murder mystery set in racially divided West Texas. The book is entitled: "Covey Jencks," which is available on Amazon. (*www.amazon.com/Covey-Jencks*)

GEM 8

GEM 9

This I know for sure:
Consumption at current levels represents a threat, locally and globally, to the natural resources on which we depend, and therefore to the wider socio-economic system. Continued growth depends on producers offering consumers a way to meet their needs and aspirations within the limits of our planet, but I am confident that business can find a way to meet these challenges in a fair, equitable and profitable way.

As a child growing up in Birmingham, Alabama, I was aware of the important role that business played in everyday life and also of the need for successful people to help those who were less fortunate. In relative terms, our family was successful. My mother was a social worker and my father was employed in aircraft manufacturing. Their influence and their outlook on the world, especially about doing good and doing the "right thing", were the genesis of my interest in corporate social responsibility (CSR).

My work in the CSR field has included serving as the head of CSR for Starbucks, which entailed working with farmers in coffee regions around the world to promote sustainable farming and equitable supply chains. My current work in promoting sustainable winemaking is a great opportunity to educate consumers on sustainable agriculture while they engage in a fun pastime. For my wine education, I obtained a Master's of Business Administration (MBA) in wine management at the Bordeaux École de Management in France. I have since published a book on the business of sustainable wine and deliver lectures on the topic around the world.

I prepared for my career by majoring in French as an undergraduate then earning a JD degree, with a focus on international law. I subsequently spent nearly 30 years in various positions — law associate, then as a diplomat, Senate staffer, and corporate executive. During this time, my work focused on international trade law and policy, as well as foreign assistance and working on important issues affecting business. These issues included South African sanctions, African policy, export controls, corporate takeovers, crisis management, ethical and sustainable supply chains, and fair-trade practices.

Collectively, my experience led me to my current and perhaps most passionate calling: promoting sustainable agriculture. At present, I am occupied – and preoccupied – with how we manage our earth's natural resources equitably. How do we feed this planet and farm responsibly, thereby ensuring the preservation of this beautiful and bountiful planet for generations to come?

As I had suspected as a child, the role of business in this and many other things is very important. Businesses can find a way to meet the challenge of sustainability and to do it in ways that are fair, equitable, and profitable. As an awareness and embrace of the principles of sustainability (economic, environmental, and social) are growing within the business sector, sustainable sourcing is becoming a point of differentiation in the marketplace.

Increasingly, responsible businesses around the world recognize that consumer behavior is a key element in any well-developed and forward-looking sustainability program. Long-term success and continued growth depend on producers offering consumers products and services that are consistent with and adhere to the principles of sustainability.

Just as the business sector is taking greater responsibility for conserving natural resources and reducing waste, consumers too, as active participants in global supply chains, must equally take responsible actions to create a more sustainable world. This is particularly important because, as the middle class expands around the globe, so do the gains in purchasing power. This will lead to much greater demand for materials, energy, and other ecosystem services.

Such demand, in turn, will likely outpace efficiency gains and overwhelm natural systems. This scenario was predicted as far back as the 18th century, when Thomas Malthus wrote *An Essay on the Principle of Population*, which raised concerns about rapidly rising populations and the negative impacts of industrialization. Such concerns have now become a reality in countries like China and India.

The signposts and statistics for the future are also troubling. The world population is expected to reach nine billion by 2050, the global middle class is expected to triple by 2030 and natural resource consumption is expected to rise to 170% of the earth's bio-capacity by 2040. The implications of these changes are dire. Sixty percent of the Earth's ecosystem services are being degraded or used unsustainably; this situation is largely driven by the growing culture of consumerism among higher-income groups.

Government policy and corporate actions are not enough. Nine billion people cannot live well and within the limits of the planet based on what can be accomplished

GEM 9

through technological innovation alone; we also need fundamental transformations of lifestyles and consumption patterns. We need wise consumers.

While many surveys show that people would like to make sustainable choices, relatively few of them adapt their behavior accordingly. The reasons for this are often related to a lack of information or to too much conflicting information and labeling; it is also a function of higher prices, higher upfront costs, and an unwillingness to act alone or to reduce convenience or product performance.

By contrast, imagine a world full of enlightened consumers in the year 2050. Such consumers would be acutely aware of the environmental and social consequences of their choices and would act to avoid negative impacts. They would also find ways to deal more easily with complex information related to products and would no longer be lost in the jungle of labels, certifications, and ingredient lists. By this time, more meaningful information would be available to consumers, and trusted brands and opinion leaders would help consumers find the best value and most sustainable solutions. Consumers, in turn, would share their insights, leading to the provision of better products and services and the disposal of products in a smarter way.

In the future, collaborative consumption would also be widespread; people would share and/or rent products and, when such products were no longer needed, they would be sold to recuperate their residual value and be reused or recycled.

Wise consumers, practicing more sustainable lifestyles and consumption patterns, will only be possible if business designs and creates products and services that are affordable and suitable to the vast majority of customers. These solutions must deliver both functional and emotional value, while also reducing their ecological footprint.

✦ ✦ ✦

GEM 9

Gem 9 Essayist: Sandra Taylor

Sandra Taylor is an internationally recognized expert with credentials in environmental and corporate responsibility, supply chain management, international trade, philanthropy, crisis management, communications and public relations, risk management, government relations, and partnerships.

Sandra's business credentials include experience with global organizations and business sectors that include: beverage, manufacturing, retail, hospitality, electronics, consumer products, agricultural commodities, natural resource industries and non-governmental organizations. Currently she is president and CEO of Sustainable Business International LLC, a consulting business that assists companies at various stages of environmental and corporate responsibility practice.

Previously, she was senior vice president with Starbucks Coffee Company in Seattle, Washington over global Corporate Responsibility, ethical procurement and the Starbucks Foundation; and Eastman Kodak Company where she led global government relations, foreign trade policy, and corporate citizenship. She has held several other senior leadership positions, including vice president of public affairs for the U.S. subsidiary of Imperial Chemical Industries Plc. (UK); international trade counsel in the U.S. Senate, and Foreign Service Officer with the U.S. State Department.

Sandra is active in community and board service, including Landesa, which seeks land rights for the poor in developing countries, Chesapeake Bay Foundation, Center for International Private Enterprise and Island Press. Sandra has had a life-long passion for winemaking and has studied wine extensively completing the French Wine Scholars course in 2010. Her first book, *The Business World of Sustainable Wine – How to Build Brand Equity in a 21st Century Wine Industry*, published in 2017. The book is available at Amazon; Barnes and Noble; and Board and Bench Publishing.

Sandra received a B.A. from Colorado Women's College in French; a JD degree from Boston University School of Law; and a MBA from the Bordeaux School of Management in France. She speaks professional French.

GEM 9

GEM 10
This I know for sure:
The impossible may just be possible!

My childhood wasn't picture-perfect.

I grew up in an impoverished South Baltimore housing project – a tough, low-income community called Cherry Hill. I shared a room and a bed with my brothers and to stay warm during the cold winter nights, my brothers and I would wrap ourselves in our winter coats and hats before going to bed. Once in bed, we would huddle close to one another, sharing each other's warmth to survive the cold of the night. The rats that had invaded our home always reminded us that we were never alone; they ravaged any food that was left unattended anywhere in our small row home. My father, despite being at heart a noble man, was so troubled with life that he drowned his troubles with excessive drinking and ended up abusing my mother more than I care to remember. The stress of this physical and emotional abuse, coupled with the tragedy of having two of her sons shipped off to the Vietnam War, ultimately led to my mother also spiraling into the pit of alcoholism.

Cherry Hill had a well-earned reputation. It was a neighborhood that outsiders dared not enter, unless accompanied by someone who lived there. Drug abuse and alcoholism were rampant and could easily become anyone's everyday reality if they were not careful. Anyone was free to walk in, but there was no guarantee that that they would ever make it out.

Living in such a challenging environment forces one to either find a way to adapt, or just give up and lean in. Fortunately for me, by day I was always an outstanding student in the classroom, but at night, it was a different story; I became a chameleon, blending into my surroundings while exploring the lifestyle of the streets. I hung out with the drug addicts, the stickup artists, the alcoholics, the gang-bangers, the purse snatchers, the glue sniffers, and the marijuana smokers. They called me "Mumbles," because I suffered from a speech impediment. My "gang" was consistently in the middle of skirmishes with the local police force, and each day would bring another near-death experience for one of us. It seemed that we were all trapped with nowhere to go, and in fact, very few of my "gang" ever made it beyond high school; most of them ended up either in prison, murdered, or addicted to drugs. It looked hopeless and breaking free seemed impossible; the world around us was crumbling, with no helping hand in sight.

Yes; this dysfunctional world was my reality. However, it became clear to me that while I was certainly *in* it, I was not necessarily *of* it.

Although I was physically trapped in this environment, spiritually, I was unbound and free and consequently, even though I lived among friends who used drugs and alcohol, and encouraged criminal activity, I began to disentangle myself from this world. Education was the key thread to pull on. Even though it was not "cool" to be smart and studious, school and reading soon became a form of escapism. Schoolwork and reading were always easy for me, so I quickly embraced them as my release and relief. When I reached high-school age, I was "strongly persuaded" to attend Baltimore Polytechnic Institute (Poly). It offered an advanced and difficult college-preparatory engineering curriculum that included calculus, analytical geometry, trigonometry, statics and dynamics, and surveying. It was the first school I had attended where folks who looked like me were in the minority. While there, I joined the football, wrestling, and track teams.

Incrementally, leaving my comfort zone helped me to see more of the world. I was exposed to new people, places, and things and the more I saw, the more I wanted to see. My vision of what I could and wanted to be became crystal clear as time went by, and mentors and helpmates began to appear out of nowhere to guide, train, and lead me into a new reality and towards a new and vibrant future – a future that included Ivy League institutions.

Two of my instructors during my junior year at Poly encouraged me to apply to the Ivy League. They had instructed me for years and were convinced that I had what it took to be successful at the highest levels of academic rigor. In fact, they were so convinced of my potential that they not only helped me with my applications, but also contributed to my application fees. At that time, I was completely oblivious as to how an Ivy League education could change my life. Given that none of my older brothers had gone to college, and that I lacked a network of family or friends who had gone to university, I would have been happy to be accepted by any university at all, let alone one of the Ivies.

Upon the advice of my mentors, I applied the University of Pennsylvania, among other leading universities. To my surprise, I was admitted to Penn's engineering program and four years later, graduated with a Bachelor of Science degree in Mechanical

GEM 10

Engineering and Applied Mechanics. From there, I attended the Amos Tuck School of Business at Dartmouth College, and received my Master of Business Administration.

I am Robert L. Wallace, aka "Mumbles." Today, I am an internationally known speaker, and founder of several award-winning technology corporations that collectively fall under the BITHGROUP umbrella of companies. My group includes an IT consulting services company (www.bithgroup.com) and Bithenergy Inc. (www.bithenergy.com), an energy services company that was recognized as the fastest-growing business on the 2015 "100 Fastest-Growing Inner City Businesses" list. Privately, through RobertWallace.com, I established EntreTeach Learning Systems LLC, which offers consulting, mentoring, and educational services to small businesses and large corporate and government clients. I am also the author of a number of books, including *Soul Food, Black Wealth, Strategic Partnerships,* and *The Ssese Principle.* Most of all, I am proud that my beautiful wife of forty years and I have raised five successful children.

It is hard to believe anything good could have come out of Cherry Hill, but it can, as my own "against all odds" success story proves. My success further shows that some of the best things in this life come from the most unlikely places. Remember: Jesus came from Nazareth, even though people thought, "Can anything good come out of Nazareth?"

When you become "comfortable being uncomfortable," anything can happen. It was "uncomfortable" for me to be ridiculed and called names because of my speech impediment, yet I embraced my discomfort and turned it into an asset. Today, I have completely overcome my speech impediment, and am asked to address audiences all over the world. Who would have thought that "Mumbles" would ever be a highly popular international speaker? I was also "uncomfortable" attending Poly, but I embraced that discomfort and went on to earn degrees from two Ivy League institutions. Crucially, this empowerment I was given has led to my lifelong efforts to help empower others.

Removing our mental, physical, and spiritual impediments allows us to see that life has so much to offer us if we dare to believe and dream. *Dreams that look impossible may be possible if you don't limit your possibilities.* If you want something different, you have to step out and do things differently. Begin to dream and work toward making your vision a reality; this is when *"the impossible may just be possible."*

✦ ✦ ✦

GEM 10

Gem 10 Essayist: **Robert Wallace**
President/CEO/Founder, Bithgroup Technologies

Robert L. Wallace is an accomplished engineer, entrepreneur, author, keynote speaker, and internationally known business consultant. Mr. Wallace is routinely sought after by the world business community. Further, he has gone on to create three successful companies - BITHGROUP Technologies, Inc., Bithenergy, Inc., and EntreTeach Learning Systems, LLC. He has authored numerous articles and books on entrepreneurship, wealth creation strategies, effective strategic partnering, intrapreneurship, and urban economic development. He earned his Master of Business Administration from Amos Tuck School of Business at Dartmouth College and graduated from the University of Pennsylvania, School of Engineering with a Bachelor of Science degree in Mechanical Engineering. (*www.bithgroup.com*)

Maryland Governor Larry Hogan has appointed Robert L. Wallace to the University Systems of Maryland Board of Regents effective July 1, 2018. The Regents oversee the system's academic, administrative, and financial operations; formulate policy; and appoint the USM chancellor and the presidents of the system's 12 institutions.

GEM 10

GEM 11

This I know for sure: *Sometimes it appears that entrepreneurial success comes out of nowhere, but that's rarely the case; it more commonly develops on a foundation of learning, prior experience, and firsthand observation.*

My seemingly "overnight success" with our "Clam Shack" restaurant and market on the eastern shore of rural Virginia was essentially four decades in the making.

I grew up in a white middle-class family in Rochester, New York where my father was an executive with a private "high quality" color printing firm and my mother was a homemaker.

It would have been expected for me to go to college, just as my three siblings and as most of my middle-class peers did, but I was a little different: I was diagnosed with dyslexia at a time when that condition was not well understood and when accommodations for it in teaching had not yet been developed. In fact, I may not have had dyslexia at all. By today's standards, it seems more likely that I had "ADD." College was not in the cards for me, so after high school, I moved to Boston, then to Cape Cod, followed by Colorado, all within the first year after completing high school.

Striking out on my own in this way took having a certain amount of confidence in myself. I gained my confidence from working on a number of after school jobs while in high school. One of my jobs was being a volunteer fireman in the suburbs of Rochester. This experience not only helped me to develop confidence in myself, it also helped me learn many things about life from the other volunteers who came from many different walks of life. I also worked at gas stations, and at other jobs, all of which were learning experiences. One of my best jobs was delivering flowers to little old ladies who were so kind to me and gave me hugs and kisses in appreciation.

When I arrived in Colorado, I was able to draw on skills I had acquired in carpentry back at home. I got a job as a carpenter working on building a condo in the Crested Butte ski area. After working for one week on the job, the carpenter union boss showed up and demanded that I show proof of having a union card, so I had to go to the union hall and "talk my" way into getting one. With my card, I was able to earn enough money to quit and buy a season pass to ski for the rest of the season.

GEM 11

After spending a year in Colorado, I hitched down to the Florida Keys and met a guy in a bar who needed someone to help him repair and deliver his boat down to St. Lucia. Though he promised to pay me $800, he didn't. While I was stranded in St. Lucia, I met an Englishman who was looking for crew to help him sail his boat to Barbados. It was a 55ft ocean cruising catamaran for Caribbean charters. I had never been on such a fast-moving boat before and could hardly keep up, but what an exciting experience it was…in every way!

While in Barbados, my new boat captain Dave advised me: "If I were you young man, I'd go to Alaska because that's where all the jobs are."

How was I going to get to Alaska? First, I had to get back to St. Lucia, which I did. When I got there, I met a beautiful woman who coincidently had just been offered a teaching job in Alaska. She asked me to go with her because she didn't want to go alone. Bingo, off we went up north.

Working in Alaska would become a fifteen year on and off experience. My work there included working in construction and in the fishing industry throughout Alaska, from the arctic to the western villages.

I took a break from working in Alaska and I moved to Hawaii for a few years. When I first arrived, I met a guy who was sailmaker. He offered me a job to be his apprentice; I worked in this capacity for six months.

Next, I replied to an advertisement to be a salesman to sell upscale "Aloha wear" to retails shops in Waikiki. I went door-to-door to virtually every retail store in Waikiki, but despite my efforts I wasn't successful because there was no market for expensive "upscale" moo moos.

With substantial selling skills in my toolkit, I next became a salesman selling fire alarms and smoke detectors door-to-door for the next two years in Hawaii. This was hard, and it was a miracle that I became one of the top salesman of the company. The challenge was that I was a white man going places where no white man had been before me. I was treading deep in the neighborhoods where I was required to make my self seem as Hawaiian as implausibly possible: where I had to change my style of clothing; change my tone of voice; and speak like a Hawaiian. This taught me an important lesson: "When you want to sell something, you have a to sell it in a way resonates with the customer."

Just to paint the picture in a little more detail of what was involved in this particular selling job, when I knocked on those doors in those neighborhoods, the person who

GEM 11

opened it "was not trying to see someone like me." My task was to first to live through it, then to win the sale because in sales, it's a zero sum game: you either win or lose.

After Hawaii, my next experience was as a door-to-door life insurance salesman in northern California. The deal here was how to convince military families that they needed this insurance? Long story, suffice it to say, it wasn't easy, and I experienced one failure after another before figuring out a formula for success. The point is, "you have to go through it to get to it" and it's way worse than it sounds. Many lessons were learned. Two more years under my belt, having sold $2.3 million per year, enough of that!

Back to Alaska. Left the wife, the car, and that whole world behind and never saw her or any of that again.

Ready for Salmon fishing in Alaska's Bristol Bay, where millions of salmon are caught every day. Between fishing and doing construction jobs every night for years, I get tired of that too.

I decided to get into the export-import business and moved to the Far East. I started in Taiwan to find something to sell. I found "headlights" (a headband with colorful lights one typically wears at parties), which I sold around Asia and throughout the world for the next two years.

For some years during this time, I made periodic visits to the eastern shore in Virginia to visit my parents who had bought some land there. Unfortunately, they both died prematurely within months of each other. I inherited the land. After years on the road, I decided to try to settle down and make something out of this "opportunity."

But, it was an opportunity to do what? With limited economic possibilities in the area, aquaculture seemed like the only possible "go to" business for me since I had some experience in the seafood business. My first endeavor entailed developing a clam and oyster hatchery that I built with my own two hands. The way this industry worked did not allow me to make enough profit because the wholesalers made all the profits. I realized that I needed to be on the retail side of the business in order to make an acceptable profit.

As a person who had by this point lived a lifetime not giving up, no matter what, I had to find a way forward. After seeing others sell products out of the back of their trucks on the highway, I decided to sell my clams in that way. It worked.

GEM 11

I decided to expand that business into a retail operation and purchased a McDonald's building that was for sale. My self-confidence led me to believe that even though McDonald's couldn't make on that stretch of highway, I could...and I did!

Had I not been able to work with my hands, and had I not had years of experience in sales, I never would have been able to create the "Clam Shack" on the eastern shore. Today, it's a million+ business that receives the highest ratings on TripAdvisor.

The moral of the story is that success may come over night, but it doesn't often. In the meantime, I advise my two sons, and every young aspiring entrepreneur, to get as many jobs as they can all the way through life because they can learn something from each job that they can use later in their entrepreneurship. Lastly, my advice is to observe other business concepts and models in use in order to discover new entrepreneurial opportunities; "stealing" someone else's idea and adapting it is fair game in business. And, if you are already in business, it's important to discover ways to grow it through constantly changing it and introducing new innovations within it.

✦ ✦ ✦

Gem 11 Essayist: **Roger Mariner**

Roger has been traveling the world since he was 18 years old. Each time he landed somewhere, he met friends, soaked up the experience and culture and moved on the next place. Over 40 years later, he is still traveling, seeking, and exploring. He has never failed to come back from his travels with a new idea, new approach, and with new friends. The reason why he travels is to refresh and to glean new perspectives that he can translate into good use in his business at the "Clam Shack" and in life. Some people went to business school to learn how to run a business; Roger learned from the school of life. Having visited most continents and countries, Roger knows firsthand that there are good ideas, good people, good business models everywhere, you just have to open your eyes, heart, and mind to perceive them. Once you have them, share them!

GEM 11

GEM 12

This I know for sure:
It's important to Always Be Creating Value (ABCV).

When I was two years old, my mother, baby brother, and I flew to America from Taiwan to join my father who was already there working to obtain his graduate degrees. Two more kids came in rapid succession before my father completed his Ph.D. course. It was fun for the kids, especially when we piled up in our little red wagon to go the park, but perhaps it wasn't as much fun for my parents. They needed help. Tag, I was it! As the oldest child, my job was to help take care of the younger kids and to be my mother's translator, as she didn't learn English until I was 10 years old. My parents would say, *"You need to pay attention, and see if something needs to be done, and just do it. Don't wait to be told."*

As a teenager, I was popular as a babysitter in the neighborhood because I knew how to take care of little babies (my youngest brother was born when I was 13). After putting the neighbor's children to bed, I looked for extra things to do like washing the dishes and picking up around the house. The parents of the children often paid me extra because I did more than they had expected. With my babysitting money, I bought many of the "extra" items that I wanted that my family couldn't afford, like contact lenses ($300 a pair back then), skis, and other things.

Fast forward, as an upper-classman engineering student at Stanford University, I saw how hard it was for entering freshmen, especially those from inner city public schools, to compete with the ones from privileged backgrounds. I volunteered to mentor these students and was instrumental in getting the university to set aside a dedicated space at the Engineering School where these and other students could study. I was so used to helping others that I was surprised when I received the "Dean of Engineering Service" Award at graduation. It turns out that my parent's advice to stay on the "look out for ways to create value" made an impression on me and served me well when I heeded it.

Over time, I realized that there are nuances around creating value. A positive one is the joy that is derived from giving value. If you enjoy helping others around you, especially those in need, such as a little old lady needing help to put her luggage in the overhead bin, your reward is the gratefulness in her eyes. When you lend a hand in this way, you are in control of that portion of your happiness that comes from creating value by serving others. This is in contrast to others who rely of external praise as a source from which to derive happiness. I fall into the former category and try to instill my value system into my sons so that they too can be in control of their happiness by ensuring that a major portion of it comes from creating value for others.

On the flip side, creating and giving value needs to be a two-way street to be sustainable. I've been in relationships with partners where my instinct was to keep giving to show my love, and when over time, I realized that the other person had not been giving much back to me, I felt unsatisfied and even resentful; inevitably, such relationships would end and the other person would be surprised. To avoid such surprises, it's important to communicate at every stage in a relationship that it must be reciprocal and that everyone needs to give and take value.

This holds true in a business relationship as well as in a personal one. In business, I have come to realize that those who do not expect and demand reciprocity are held in lower esteem. If you just give and give and expect nothing in return, you are considered a fool, as I learned when I started my consulting company in mid-2000's. Our focus was on helping start-ups in Silicon Valley with their marketing strategies. One of my best friends, who was an investor, asked around about what people thought of me. She was told that I wasn't that smart. She shared that finding with me and I was shocked because some of those who had communicated that message to her were some of the very people I had helped. The investor then clarified the situation and explained that yes, I was very smart about marketing, but I considered was dumb about business and the proof of that was that I had helped those people for free and had never asked for any remuneration despite the lengths I had gone to help them. Wow.

Now, as I deliver entrepreneurship and innovation programs around the world, a major theme of my teaching is about "creating and *exchanging* value." I also underscore that every start-up needs to have a compelling value proposition to succeed.

A major step is to understand the market and the customer: "What are their needs and problems and how can a solution be created that is valuable in meeting their needs and solving their problems?"

Understanding the marketplace and the customer is not as easy, however. A perfect example is found in a story from the 1960's that involves General Mills. This company's research led it to the conclusion that Japanese love sweets and assumed that Japanese housewives would therefore eagerly embrace the cake mixes that it produced. To the company's surprise, its major Japan cake-mix marketing campaign was a resounding

GEM 12

failure and no one bought the cake mixes. Little did the firm know that Japanese kitchens did not have ovens so the housewives didn't have the equipment to bake cakes. Thus, while the company had done some research, in this case, just enough to identify the need; they hadn't done enough to understand *how* to meet the need in the environment.

How you are attempting to "create value" matters. Product market-fit is about understanding the customer and building a solution that has value because it appropriately fills a gap and meets a need. Entrepreneurs who are successful create the "right" value. Perhaps there is no better example of this than that of Steve Jobs. Believe it or not, he often visited the Apple store that was located a few blocks from his home in Palo Alto, California. While there, he observed customers at great length. From his observations and interpretations of them, he realized that older people were intimidated by computers and laptops. Having spotted this "need", he spent several years designing the iPad in a way that would meet such needs. It's no accident that the iPad was a success from the outset; it was designed for success.

Creating "true value" starts with having the "right" mindset. Such a mindset seeks to create value as broadly as possible, not just by providing a single product or service. The notion of creating "broad" value entails seeking to create value for all stakeholders in a value chain. Andrew Mason, for instance, who is the founder of Groupon, is an excellent example of an entrepreneur who created "broad" value. He designed Groupon to create value for consumers, merchants, employees, investors, and even for himself. This "360 value" creation perspective helped Groupon reach a billion dollar valuation in less than two years, making it one of the fastest start-ups to do so.

I know for sure that to be successful in any size business, it is incumbent upon entrepreneurs to embrace the notion that they must *Always Be Creating Value* in all that they do. When they adopt this mindset in business, and in their personal lives, they will not only be successful in business, they will also be happy as human beings.

✦ ✦ ✦

GEM 12

Gem 12 Essayist: **Gigi Wang**

Gigi Wang runs a consulting firm, MG-Team, LLC, which delivers entrepreneurship and innovation programs and services for international business development globally. She is also an Industry Fellow & Faculty at UC Berkeley Sutardja Center for Entrepreneurship where she teaches a start-up boot-camp and executive innovation programs. She advises and mentors dozens of start-ups from around the world. Clients have included SAP, Amsterdam Center for Entrepreneurship, Grupo Aguia Branca (Brazil), NATO, Ecole d' Ponts Business School, Japan External Trade Organization (JETRO), SRI International, Verizon Wireless, Lagardere, and numerous universities and global incubators.

Before starting up MG-Team, Ms. Wang was on the executive teams of a number of tech start-ups in wireless, software, hardware, and services. As an Internet pioneer in the 90's, she started up Pacific Internet in Singapore (IPO on NASDAQ in 1999) and launched the internationally renowned TRUSTe Internet privacy program in 1996.

Gigi holds BS and MS degrees in Mechanical Engineering from Stanford University where she was President of the Tau Beta Pi Engineering Honor Society, and a MBA from the Haas School of Business at UC Berkeley. She is a frequent speaker at entrepreneur and innovation conferences around the world including the World Investment Conference, Food Executive Europe, Silicon Valley Comes to the Baltics, IBM Global Start-Up Camp, and Global R&D Conference.

As a child, she first emigrated from Taiwan, to Canada (Nova Scotia), then to the U.S., first to North Dakota and then to Michigan where she grew up, before moving to California for college. She has two sons, Max (25) who is an engineer, and Zac (21) who is studying physics in college. Gigi has been playing co-ed soccer for over 25 years, and has recently taken up golfing. She and her partner, John, live in the Bay area and love to cook cuisines from around the world for their family and friends.

GEM 12

GEM 13

This I know for sure:
We have needs and we have wants. I enjoy building off the magic that comes when they intersect.

If you ask a question in the right way and are a good listener, you will hear about what people really want. Give people what they want and problems are solved, right? Not so fast. We are ill-advised to blindly indulge our desires; too many of us would get into trouble! Usually, we have to temper wants with actual needs. Knowing how to balance the fine line between them is what intrigues me.

Who am I? A middle aged guy, a father of two girls who take my breath away, and a husband to the smartest and most patient woman I know. I am also the son of proud parents who schooled me well, a sibling who tries hard to be supportive, and a citizen who is deeply concerned for the fate of our people, and I mean all people with twenty-three chromosomal pairs.

While my current business is cake and confections, it was preceded by a short stint as a lawyer, which was inspired by my work in health education. My goal in becoming a lawyer was to have the credentials that would qualify me to stand before school boards and PTAs to address the glaring gap between what the curriculum materials thought students "needed" to know versus what they in fact "wanted" to know. That was a big ask and way bigger than I was prepared for.

Before I attended law school, and well before I was a professional baker, I was a health educator. I taught the basics of reproduction at community clinics and was a guest lecturer in high schools, colleges, and at professional conferences. I also conducted workshops and provided counseling about sexual assault. I learned that not everyone is or wants to be sexually active but everyone wants information. Most want to know about their bodies and about those of others, and they want to discuss their feelings and share emotions in a safe space. There are a lot of wants, but there was plenty of need too.

Establishing credibility with the audience was the key to successful communication. For high school lectures, the problem was that the instructional materials were so out of touch with reality that everything felt contrived. So, I improvised a peer education exercise to conclude my five-day lesson plan that was very effective. It required students to anonymously write down questions on papers, which I pulled from a box to answer in a group setting. I asked students to answer the questions and stood ready to supplement their answers. Talk about a lively discussion! Everyone paid attention.

GEM 13

It was the perfect opportunity to inform them of their "needs" while addressing what they "wanted" to know.

I think about that job all of the time. The experience greatly shaped my perspective of how people deal with the reconciliation of their needs and wants. I still wonder where we're going with sex education in this country? I note, however, that many issues about sexuality, harassment, and abuse are increasingly being brought into the open, but we have a long way to go. At least now, young people can turn to the Internet as a resource for answering questions about sex.

The energy between what people want versus what people need drives a lot of things in our society by creating conflict and resolution. When you take a step back and really listen, you can see that people are not alone in what they are searching for and there are more similarities than differences in these aims and goals.

It took me almost losing my business to fully appreciate how deeply it was rooted in bringing together the needs and wants of people. Maybe that should have been obvious to me before I opened my first bakery, but honestly I stumbled into being an entrepreneur. At the time, I am not sure I knew what an entrepreneur was. It turns out that if you are innovative and like staying busy then you are probably an entrepreneur at heart. All I knew is that I wanted to bake. It began as a New Year's resolution, evolved into a side business, then just blossomed.

When the economy slowed down in 2009, I had to make a decision about my business. It was getting by but things had to change. So I went to fans and critics alike for feedback. My staff and I posed important questions, but the most important responses came when we just listened to them gab. Two key messages emerged: "I **need** something portable", and "I really just **want** your cream cheese frosting." There it was: needs and wants.

Their responses surprised me. It was great information that I had no idea how to use. Sometimes you can sense that there is an opportunity but it's not clear how to seize it and you don't know if it's bankable or bonk. I wondered how I would develop a product concept out of it, how to market and sell it, and how to build a business around it. I knew it would take years of work. To create this new opportunity, I would have to change everything about my current operations, which also meant closing our retail storefronts. This was a very high mountain that I wasn't sure I wanted to climb. On the one hand, I wanted to embrace change but on the other I longed for the familiar. I realized that change is inevitable, however, and it sometimes comes slowly and with great effort.

GEM 13

I wasn't ready to quit the business world, but I didn't know if pivoting to the new product concept would be worth the effort. In my first business, something we did worked, but I realized that I needed to understand more about what that was exactly and how to capture the essence of that success to recreate another one.

To gain perspective I stopped focusing on myself and focused on listening to my customers. I let my mind drift back to when I was a health educator, when it was all about "needs" and "wants" and so I was listening for that.

What emerged as a result was "cake in a jar," which is our main line of business today. The business is stronger and better than before and I have more time to listen and create. My efforts to satisfy my customers' needs and wants helped me meet my own. Every time I think about it, it feels like magic.

✦ ✦ ✦

Gem 13 Essayist: **Warren Brown**

The owner of the Washington, DC-based Countertop Productions, Inc., CakeLove, and the former host of the Food Network's *Sugar Rush*, Warren Brown is an entrepreneurial icon. Taking an unconventional career path, he left his job as an attorney to pursue his passion: baking cakes.

Brown founded his first bakery, CakeLove, in 2002 and fell in love with a relentless pursuit of perfecting his recipe for success. He is the author of four cookbooks in which he reveals his baking secrets and time saving tips in the kitchen.

Brown continues to innovate in the bakery space to grow his business and influence trends in snacks and packaged desserts. His latest creations are cake in a jar packaged under two different brands CakeLove and Don't Forget Cake! He also has a line of healthy snacks under the brand Spark Bites. Each are sold through major retailers through the United States.

Warren Brown has been recognized for his entrepreneurial spirit by local and national media including *The Oprah Winfrey Show, The Today Show*, NPR, CNN, and *Inc.* magazine. He has been featured in national advertisement campaigns for American Express and in numerous books on career change. He lives in Washington, D.C. with his wife and two daughters.

GEM 13

GEM 14

This I know for sure:
You must find your passion(s) and ways to pursue them. Hopefully, you can make them your profession, but if not, you can integrate them into your life.

Growing up, I never was totally sure what exactly my Dad did as his "day job." I knew that he had gone to medical school for a couple of years in Europe when he couldn't attend medical school in the United States, but that he hadn't completed his studies. I knew that he worked at Mt. Sinai hospital in New York for a while, then at the University of Maryland, and that he sometimes wore what looked like a white lab coat.

However, what I did know was where he was going and what he was doing when he donned his tennis clothes and gathered his racket and balls, or when he asked me to "cue his lines" when he was playing a part in Hamlet, or Othello, Antigone, or John Brown's Body. He was happiest at those times, particularly when he came home from a tennis tournament with a trophy or came home pumped with adrenaline after a performance at Arena Stage, the Washington Theater Club, or from the summer stock at Wellfleet, Massachusetts – or even after filming a movie. Tennis and acting were his passions. His day job clearly was not.

My mother had dreams for me, the only girl and the eldest of three children. She loved the English language and foreign languages, international travel, and ballet. She instilled in me a passion for these things and encouraged me to read and to study. I began studying Spanish at public school in third grade and developed an interest in other cultures. She facilitated international travel opportunities for me at a young age and enrolled me in a very serious ballet school.

My parents were first-generation college graduates who met at university. They both came from very small towns and families of limited means, but dared to travel to Europe as a first foreign adventure; not as tourists, but to live. Dad lived and studied in Switzerland and Mom joined him in Germany for his second year of medical school. When I was just nine years old, she arranged for me to spend a summer in Mexico City with a Mexican teacher she had befriended during a trip she had taken there. (The teacher was killed in a car crash the day I was to depart and someone had the presence of mind to contact my family to forewarn them not to put me on the plane.) When I was 16, I travelled to Spain with a group of junior high school students from the school where my mom taught English. My evening and weekend ballet study required

GEM 14

her to take me on a bus three days a week, going from one side of the city to the opposite end, for several years until I was old enough to go alone.

My Dad pursued his passions and served as an example to help me find my own. Mom exposed me to new ideas and experiences and facilitated and guided me on a path to identifying and pursuing my passions. She encouraged me to see the world, to pursue a profession that would incorporate my passions (she suggested that I become a stewardess), to remain focused on my ballet while maintaining my grades in school, as my Dad would not allow me to go to ballet class unless my grades were stellar. This path was not the norm for a young African-American woman a half-century ago.

I have been immersed in global issues since I can remember. I was an activist in college participating in the anti-apartheid movement. I marched every African Liberation Day, joined a Marxist-Leninist Mao Tse Tung Thought (MLMTT) study group, spent my junior semester in Madrid when Francisco Franco died and Spain was undergoing a major political transformation. I joined the Foreign Service straight out of undergraduate school and lived in the Dominican Republic and Mexico as a single (younger than most) woman of color.

My post-foreign-service professional career has included advising over 20 foreign countries on issues ranging from normalizing diplomatic relations, lifting sanctions, supporting trade agreements and simply navigating the U.S. body politic. I have advocated for U.S. private-sector interests abroad and for foreign companies seeking investment in the United States, supporting foreign direct investments. I am a registered foreign agent and lobbyist, terms abhorred by many, abused by some and misunderstood by most, both Americans and foreigners. I have been mentored by some of the best in their professions and have now taken on the role of being a mentor to many others. I was a presidential appointee of President Clinton, to the position of Assistant Secretary and Director General of the U.S. and Foreign Commercial Service at the Department of Commerce under the late Secretary Ron Brown, my friend and mentor. Ironically, I was sworn in after being confirmed by the U.S. Senate, about a year after my Dad retired from the Department of Commerce's National Oceanic and Atmospheric Administration. Finally, I became clear about what his day job was!

On a C-130 aircraft, from Dubrovnik to Dover, Delaware, I accompanied Ron Brown's casket and those of 32 friends, employees, crew, journalists and corporate executives killed in a plane during a trade mission to Bosnia and Croatia in 1996; the trip on which he was killed was the only trip I did not travel with him in the last six months of his life.

While many of these activities are life-changing, fulfilling, enriching and admirable accomplishments, they only feed one side of the brain. What truly feeds my passion is dance. What brings me peace, keeps me grounded, reminds me of the importance of physical and mental agility, is ballet.

I studied ballet throughout all of my formative years, at a ballet school founded by two African-American women from Boston. I went on to dance with the Capitol Ballet and the Vassar Dance Theater. I studied with the Dance Theater of Harlem and performed with Ballet Santo Domingo. I took jazz and contemporary dance classes several times a week for years.

Sadly, my dance activities ceased for about 18 years when I was preoccupied with life's challenges and opportunities – marriage, raising stepchildren and the daughter I gave birth to, and working, working, working and working. I was a rare spectator at dance performances during that period; it was too difficult to watch. I lost sight of this critical passion, which had been the foundation of what made me successful and which had taught me discipline, perseverance, musicality and strength. Dance had fed my soul.

While my passion for things international was integral to my professional life, ballet had always filled a unique space. With a mastery of Barre and center floor progressions, the French terminology, self-awareness and a love of the art form, I realized that I could take a ballet class anywhere in the world and feel challenged and fulfilled. I have taken adult classes two to three times a week at home or wherever I travel for the last five years. I learned that the physical and mental discipline is never lost, even if physical limitations develop over time

Nothing is more soothing to me than taking a ballet class. When I do, I leave feeling rejuvenated, having enjoyed the classical music and the instruction. I depart drenched in sweat and content that I still can find that special place, that escape from everything and everyone for the 90 minutes that is the standard duration of a class. Re-engaging with that lifelong comfort zone, that space of passion, allows me to emerge better able to handle all else that is going on in my life.

✦ ✦ ✦

GEM 14

Gem 14 Essayist: Honorable Lauri Fitz-Pegado

A partner at the Livingston Group, she leads the international, education and non-profit practices. She has represented over 20 countries and many corporations to support issues including normalizing diplomatic relations, lifting trade sanctions and facilitating investment. She served as an Assistant Secretary and Director General of Commerce during President Clinton's administration managing 130 offices overseas and 90 in the United States facilitating services to help small and medium sized companies export and advocating for major U.S. companies competing for foreign contracts. She led the Global Gateway Management and Corporate Affairs and Communications departments for Iridium, LLC, a global satellite and paging company. She was a managing director at Hill and Knowlton and an executive at Gray and Company for over a decade. Lauri Fitz-Pegado served as a diplomat in the Dominican Republic and Mexico. She performed with the Dominican Ballet Company and taught ballet in Mexico City. A Washington, DC native, she attended Jones-Haywood School of Ballet with the support of a Ford Foundation Scholarship through the School of American Ballet and danced with the Capitol Ballet Company. A trustee on the boards of Global Communities and the Chesapeake Bay Foundation, she is an advisor to the Women in Public Policy Project, the Ron Brown Scholars, and the International Career and Advancement Program at the Aspen Institute. She is a member of the Council on Foreign Relations and the Washington Government Relations Group. Fitz-Pegado graduated cum laude with Phi Beta Kappa honors from Vassar College and has a Master of Arts in International Affairs from the School of Advanced International Studies at Johns Hopkins University. She enjoys a family of three children and four grandchildren on three continents, speaks Spanish and Portuguese and takes ballet classes as often as possible.

GEM 14

GEM 15

This I know for sure:
You must learn how to learn before you can master yourself and your fate.

I learned this the hard way, and later in life.

I grew up in Philadelphia at a time when schools were segregated, when many African American households were poor and few had fully functioning, live-in fathers. Fortunately, this was not the case in our household. Our father never touched a drop of alcohol and worked every day, as did my mother; they also worked together in entrepreneurial endeavors. They came up from the South in the great migration to the North; hoping to experience great things in life, they shared not only their material things with us, but also their hopes, aspirations, and dreams.

As a result, I was inspired by my parents. I did well in school and felt emotionally rewarded when I acquired and was able to leverage knowledge. This set me apart from most of my classmates, of which there were about a thousand in high school. As a result, I thought I was really smart and rarely did my homework. I excelled by listening with absolute concentration to what the teachers were saying so that I did not have to study. This habit of laser-focused listening would serve me well in later life.

I did not really know how to learn until I attended graduate school at Carnegie-Mellon University (CMU). I mention the school simply because its name sends chills down the spines of those who know about its quantitative focus. However, having previously attended CMU as an undergraduate (sailing through the experience and acquiring two degrees in three-and-a-half years), I was in no way scared of its reputation.

When I returned to CMU to attend graduate school, it was another story – and it was a story told entirely in math. School suddenly became scary. Ever heard of upper and lower case Greek symbols in equations? Well, neither had I.

I found myself in classes with a bunch of mathematical geniuses, and I was not one of them. I went to the computer lab with one of those geniuses one day, with my massive stack of FORTRAN batch cards. I found that I had two problems. Firstly, I did not know how to type. This was because, when I was in my segregated school in Philadelphia, students who were deemed to "have promise" were not allowed to learn typing (no doubt due to a lack of typewriters) – it was only taught to girls who were expected to become typists. Secondly, worse than the problem of not being able to type (which

GEM 15

itself was a serious problem in the batch-card world, because incorrectly punched typed cards meant that the whole system would not compute), I fundamentally had no idea how to program, what I was programming, or why I was programming it.

The genius I had accompanied over to the freezing cold computer building made a *single* programming error and broke down and cried (I had so many errors, I could not even count them). I told her: "If you didn't know what I don't know, you'd kill yourself." At that moment, I knew I would make it in life because I could stand in the midst of my complete ignorance and yet view it as only a temporary state.

When it came time to learn operations research and the simplex method (which I could not understand) I had to see what I was made of. So, I acquired as many books as I could on these topics – figuring that, by reading them all, I would somehow learn the subject matter. It took, on average, about five books on each topic, which, due to their weight, were excruciatingly heavy to carry to the library each day (no car and no Internet, of course). As a result of carrying so many books, I still have the callouses on my hands to this day.

I went to the dreary basement in the school library, faced my chair to the white wall, studied, and prayed to learn. Minute by minute, hour by hour, day by day, and for weeks on end, I studied. Finally, I had a breakthrough and actually learned something; I moved from utter ignorance to actually understanding my first few nuggets in the foundation of knowledge on the topic. Hallelujah, I was beginning to see the light!

Do you have any idea of how hard it is to learn something when you know nothing at all about it? Imagine staring at Chinese characters on a page. Just because you are looking at them does not mean you understand them if you have no knowledge of the Chinese language. Well, that is what it was like.

The important lesson I learned from this was not about operations research; rather, it was that I could learn all by myself – just me and the books. The secret formula was: "Face the wall, have no distractions, and bring tons of reference books. Have no sound, no music, and no windows to look out of – just study." In my work as a consultant, I have consistently applied the "face the white wall and shut out the world" technique of learning as my starting point when I need to tackle complex and unfamiliar problems.

Over time, I have learned to estimate how long it is likely to take me to go from zero knowledge to a competent understanding in a given domain. It is just like the old TV game that required contestants to estimate how many notes of a song they would have to hear before they could name the song and declare, "I can name that tune in five notes." Being able to "call it" requires an ability to hear and perceive the significance of each note and its role in the song.

In a business context, this translates into processing every bit of information at one's disposal. When pitching to a new potential client in person, for instance, it is important to be able to process information from small clues that show on a person's face – eye movement, a lip quiver, or a crease in a brow. As a consultant who subscribes to the ABS principle ("always be selling"), it is important to gauge whether I will be able to land a potential client or not. When I ask the ABS questions, I watch everything in the person's face and body language in order to "call it."

This is why it is maddening to talk to people while they are looking down at their cell phones; you are not able to see the whites of their eyes, from which a great deal of information can be gleaned. Apparently, the big leap between primates and humans occurred when it was possible to see the whites of the primates' eyes; this enabled the reading, sensing, and interpretation of information that was critical for survival.

I tried the "look into his eyes" technique at an important juncture in my consulting life. There was a senior boss at the World Bank who was suspected of double crossing our consulting team on something we were working on with locals in an African country. The double cross only became apparent when, after months of working together with many locals, the counterpart head of the local team (who had agreed on our unified position) suddenly, at the presentation with the big boss, went in the exact opposite direction. We immediately knew that the local person had been "turned" by the big boss.

On the way home on the airplane, the big boss sat behind me. I knew I had one chance to see if he had double crossed us. So, I went up to him and said: "May I ask you a question?" I let the question hang in the air for a few seconds while I watched him squirm. His eyes danced and his lips curled, and only then did I ask: "Do you have an aspirin?"

In the slight moment it took him to answer, I had received and processed all of the information I needed. The big boss was so relieved that all I was asking for was an aspirin and not the truth.

The main takeaway is that it is important to know how many "notes" you need of the tune in order to "call it." Crucially, be sure to count the notes that manifest as sights, sounds, and movements, as well as those that are presented as hard data.

GEM 15

Importantly, know when it is time to face the "white wall of learning" and put in the hard work. When you are not working with much else, it is your own laser-focused concentration that will be your savior, enabling you to "call it."

✦ ✦ ✦

Gem 15 Essayist: **Sharon T. Freeman, Ph.D.**

Dr. Freeman is an entrepreneur and business owner who established her first consulting firm in Hong Kong in 1985, where she lived for 12 years. She is the President & CEO of Gems of Wisdom Consulting, Inc. and the author and publisher of 25 books, including this one; her library can be found on Amazon and on www.gemsofwisdomconsulting.com. She has worked in over 100 countries during the past 30+ years, and serves as an appointed Advisor to the Secretary of Commerce and the U.S. Trade Representative on trade policy matters. She is also the Chair of the U.S. Trade Representative's Trade Advisory Committee on Africa (TACA). She also previously served on the Advisory Boards of the U.S. Export Import Bank, the U.S. Energy Department, the U.S. Small Business Administration, and on the Board of the DC Chamber of Commerce. She is the current Vice Chair of the Montgomery County Charter Commission.

She is the wife of Peter Hagos Gebre, and the proud mother of Negash Gebre, author of the Afterword of this book. As an expert on ecosystems for promoting the growth of entrepreneurship around the world, and as an expert on minority business development, exporting, and regulatory compliance, her services have been retained by leading development institutions, corporations, foreign countries, and others for over three decades. She frequently speaks about important issues in trade and business on behalf of the U.S. State Department around the world and publishes articles about her work on LinkedIn. She holds undergraduate and graduate degrees from Carnegie-Mellon University and a Ph.D. in Applied Management and Decision Sciences from Walden University.

GEM 15

GEM 16

This I Know for sure:
Everybody needs to travel through life with a road dog!

In the management science domain, you'd call a "road dog" a mentor or advisor. Where I grew up In Youngstown, Ohio, we'd call him or her an "ace boon coon buddy" (or informant). Essentially, a "road dog" is someone who helps you find a way and aids you in making your way. That person can show you the way because s/he knows the way and has traveled that road before. Your "road dog" is also your cheerleader as you travel on your road in life.

The "road dog" sniffs out danger on the road, sees things clearly for you when you have blurry vision; tells you where the landmines are; and listens for you when you can only hear; s/he also handles matters on your behalf that you cannot gracefully address. The critical thing is that the "road dog" must be on "the" road; it's a road that you have determined but is one that you don't necessarily know how to navigate. It has many twists and turns, byways and highways, and your "dog" is the one who is in the position to tell you to slow down on this part of the road, go faster on that part, and watch out for the treacherous drop off on the curve ahead.

When you don't have a "road dog" you can get in a lot of trouble. Take the case of the recent forced resignation of the newly appointed Washington, D.C. Public School Chancellor of Education. He blew into town from Oakland, California and didn't have any "road dogs" in Washington. Consequently, he made one fatal error very early, which he never would have made if he had a "road dog" because his "dog" would have advised him against skirting the rules to get his daughter into a preferred school. His "dog" would have sniffed out that danger and advised him against his ill-fated march of folly.

There's always a "dog" on the side of the road, the challenge is recognizing him or her. The person may come in any form, be old or young, or be outside or inside your race. Those who succeed in life are always on the lookout for them and engage them at every stage in life.

Early on when we are young our parents serve as our "road dogs", but often we can't recognize them as such and are resistant to their advice; we think they are just trying to control our lives. Once we move beyond that stage and begin to recognize

GEM 16

their advice as sage, we then begin the process of transitioning to the next stage of adulthood in our lives where we value and leverage their counsel.

For many in black communities, grandmothers play a critical "road dog" role because they are wise and also because there is less resistance to accepting their advice. In fact, the role grandmothers play in this regard is so important in the black community that a well-researched study once concluded that black women live longer because they couldn't afford to die because they were needed so much.

My best friend when I was growing up was Bob Billingslea. He was raised by his grandparents. Even though I was young, I recognized that he was my "road dog" quite simply because I knew he had been on the road. Unlike me, who was stuck at home studying all the time, he was into music and frequented night clubs and cool hangout places in "the hood." When I was able to break away, he took me on the road with him. While I wasn't as cool as him, I got special points in his household because his grandfather always said, "Bobby, you need to be like 'Normie', he's going to make something of himself one day." Bob did make something of himself as well, and ended his career as a Vice President at Disney.

In my time, with parents who came up north from the south, there was no "playing" around about staying on the straight and narrow. If you looked like you were going the wrong way, if you were in the north they'd send you down south to get your head together, and if you were in the south, they'd send you up north. If you didn't get it together after that you'd be out on your own, pure and simple. My mother, like most during that time and circumstances, used to say: "I brought you into the world, and I will take you out!

Being thus dutifully on the straight and narrow path, I went to university, as expected, and continued until I earned a terminal degree. Earning a Ph.D. at that time in the early 1960s as a black student was a rarity. When I was in graduate school earning a master's degree at Ohio State University, a young professor advised me to aim even higher and go for a Ph.D. That professor and his wife were a young Amish couple who saw the potential in my work and encouraged me and showed me the way. I said to myself, "what is a Ph.D.?" I asked my father and he said, "All I know is that you better get a real job and make some money to support yourself." My mother, who also didn't know what a Ph.D. was very happy about me pursuing it, whatever it was.

I went back to my professor and asked one critical question: "If I get a Ph.D. will they call me doctor?" He said yes, and I said, "count me in."

GEM 16

I was an ROTC cadet in college and therefore owed the Army three years upon graduation. On active duty, I held the rank of First Lieutenant. After basic training, I was assigned to manage a recruitment and induction center. This is where I met my first post-college road dog. He held the rank of E-9. He was a white NCO under no obligation to help me BUT HE DID. One morning he said "Lt. Johnson, there are only two ways to do your military time, the hard way or the easy way." He added, "if you let me, I'll show you the smart way". It dawned on me that there was no way, not even in the military, to be successful as a junior officer without the support of an "NCO road dog."

From my time in the military and throughout my civilian life, I have made it my business to locate and keep one or two "road dogs" close. I found them everywhere, and especially in my fraternity, Omega Psi Phi, which has been a rich source for me to identify "road dogs". Many that I have had over the years are still traveling successfully with me today. Sadly, my first "road dog", Bob, passed away after traveling on the road with me for 70 years.

Aside for a brief stint working in Pittsburgh's poverty program, I have spent most of my career in academia, as a professor, trying to be a "road dog" for students, especially for black male students. Some students listened, some didn't. One thing I learned for sure is that none succeeded without acquiring a "road dog". Having one enables one to see beyond one's own sight and enables one to take the road… "less traveled by, and that has made all the difference."

✦ ✦ ✦

GEM 16

Gem 16 Essayist: **Norman Johnson, Ph.D.**

Norman J. Johnson is a Vice President at ALISIAS, a public policy, policy relations firm. His immediate past position was Professor of Organizational Science at the School of Business and Industry, Florida A&M University. Before Florida A&M, he was at Georgia Tech (GT). While at GT, he was a member of the general faculty and served as a Senior Executive in the Office of the President (1988-1998) and held three portfolios: Marketing, Minority Affairs, and Change Management. In the minority affairs portfolio, he redesigned and redirected Georgia Tech's nationally recognized and acclaimed engineering effort OMED, building on the Carnegie-Mellon Action Project called CMAP, where he was its first director.

He earned his master's and Ph.D. from the Ohio State University, where he specialized in education leadership (MS) and organizational behavior (Ph.D.). He further studied at the Harvard Law and Business Schools. He has held faculty appointments at the University of Illinois at Chicago, University of Pittsburgh, Carnegie-Mellon University, Florida A&M University, and the Georgia Institute of Technology. Sandwiched between the GT and Florida A&M University assignments, was a three-year engagement at the Honeywell Corporation in Minneapolis, MN in the training division. In the late 1960s, he joined the co-founding team of the School of Urban and Public Affairs at Carnegie Mellon and served as the first Associate Dean (1969-1981) of its nationally recognized master's program in Management and Public policy.

Currently, he is a member of the National Academy of Public Administration (NAPA), where for the last seven years he has served as chair of the Brownlow Book Award Committee. He also serves as a member of NAPA's Board of Directors. Previously, he served as an elected member of the Atlanta Public School Board and was a member of the twelve member Steering Committee of the Council of Urban Boards of Education (CUBE). He holds life membership in the NAACP, Omega Psi Phi Fraternity, and the 100 Black Men of Atlanta. He is past president of the National Association of Schools of Public Affairs and Administration, the Atlanta School Board, and past chair of the Board of Trustees at the Mt. Ararat Baptist Church, Pittsburgh, PA where he learned best practices in volunteerism in non-profit settings.

GEM 17

This I know for sure:
"The Right Plant in the Right Place OR It's Not All about You."

Later in life, I happen to take up gardening. In many ways, I learned that gardening is a lot like life—not only because it involves living things, but also because successful gardening involves a macrocosm of life itself.

There are many aphorisms for success in gardening. One of the most prominent is: "right plant in the right place." That is, a sun-loving plant will die (or fail to thrive) in a shady location and a shade-loving plant will die in a sunny location. The success of a plant, however beautiful and vigorous, depends on its nature and the circumstances under which it is grown.

Many successful people believe that their success is attributable to their talents and efforts alone. But just as plants need the right conditions in which to thrive, people also need them in their work: if you're in the wrong job, the wrong company, or in the wrong circumstances, your career will suffer or at least fail to thrive, just like a sun loving plant in the shade.

In my own example, for 10 years after graduating from undergraduate university, I prepared for what I hoped would be an exceptional career. I worked for two years as an engineer, attended and graduated from business school after two years, then worked for four years writing patent applications for a Fortune 20 company, while I earned a law degree. Despite all of my hard work and talent, my career was sabotaged by circumstances and I was left in the shade.

I was excited to accept a marketing position with a Fortune 10 company in its management development program (MDP). It turned out that my first assignment in the MDP was a first-level "marketing" position consisting of selling communications services to the federal government. It was supposed to be a training position in preparation for a second-level assignment within two years.

Even though I was 30 years old at the time, and had experience in a variety of workplace circumstances (engineering, law), I was in for some real hard lessons about 1980s corporation life. Talented or not, hard-working or not, MDP or not, one of the most important aphorisms in life is: **it is important that your boss likes you and wants you to succeed.**

GEM 17

During this two-year, first-level assignment, my particular white boss showed in a number of ways, that he didn't like me. Not least, he would make sexual insinuations about me and the black department secretary. Maybe he just wanted to take this insolent, over-educated black boy down a peg or two, to put him in his place. I certainly didn't get the feeling that he wanted me to succeed. I'm sure he wouldn't have done this (sexual insinuations) with someone (white) that he liked and wanted to succeed.

After, many months and dozens of incidents, and after he wouldn't stop his sexual insinuations about the secretary, I finally blew up and "expressed my displeasure" in forceful and off-color, terms. Soon thereafter, I was fired. Actually, I didn't even connect the dots until years later, after I retired and was looking back on how my career had derailed.

By contrast, during this nostalgic review of my career, I remembered my last job teaching business law and other business subjects at a local college and thought how different it was. My black boss showed in a number of ways that I was welcome and appreciated, despite the obvious displeasure of my white colleagues, who wouldn't have hired me had the choice been theirs.

With the help, support, and "protection" of my black boss, I thrived in this position for the last 25 years of my career. If I would have had such a supportive and encouraging boss at the "start" of my career, in my first-level MDP assignment, my career might have been, would have been, much more successful.

A boss can like you and want you to succeed for myriad reasons: for example, because you are like him/her in some way; because you remind him/her of himself in similar circumstances in his/her life; because you are attractive in some way (e.g., tall); because you are unusually competent; or because your success is a measure of his/her performance.

So, like the sun plant that has too much shade or the shade plant that has too much sun, I believe success may not be a matter of just your talent and hard work, it's often also a matter of circumstances and environment. In my case, and that of many others, positive circumstances often involve the presence or absence of a mentor—a supervisor or some other superior who takes your success as his or her duty and responsibility.

My takeaway, based on my experience is, environment and circumstances are key to your success. So first before accepting a job, try to find out the reputation of the organization. This is something they didn't teach in business school (but they could

GEM 17

have), probably because the typical business school professor is an academician. Professors generally, never study the true determinants of success after business school. Use all the resources that are available to you in vetting the reputation of the firm. If you don't like the results of your investigation, then at your job interview try to ask questions to clarify issues. Generally, you don't want to work for a company or organization with a bad reputation that will unduly affect your rise to the top.

Second, try to find out the circumstances under which the employee you will be replacing left the company: You don't want a boss that will take you "from the frying pan into the fire." Ask to speak privately to current employees under your prospective boss and ask questions about his management style—in particular, about his/her mentoring capability. Your key to success in an organization is to choose the right boss, or the best boss available, or come as close to it as you can.

Third, in a more affirmative vein, if after all your preventive efforts in environment and circumstances, you find yourself in a less-than-ideal environment, under a less-than-ideal boss, be assertive and strategic in responding to negative inputs. If I had reported the behavior of my boss to HR, instead of responding in kind, I would have been on much firmer ground to eliminate his provocations. But, that was a different time.

Still, there are other ways to respond to less than ideal environments and bosses, you have but to investigate the myriad articles and books on the subject. My advice is: "An ounce of prevention is worth a pound of cure."

◆ ◆ ◆

GEM 17

Gem 17 Essayist: **Bruce McGee**

Bruce McGee retired after 30 years as a college professor at various Maryland educational institutions. During his tenure as a professor, he taught subjects as varied as Business Law and Statistics, Marketing and Quantitative Methods, and Accounting and Corporate Finance.

Professor McGee came by this ability to teach such heterogeneous subject matter through his amazingly diverse education. After completing an electrical engineering degree at George Washington University in Washington, D.C., he worked as a design engineer at the Westinghouse Electric Company where he contributed to the AWACS (Airborne Warning and Control System).

Being quite an ambitious man, at Westinghouse, he learned that an engineer with a management degree would be even more employable. So, after an extensive search for a quantitative business school, Professor McGee was granted an educational leave of absence from Westinghouse and was accepted to a two-year program at the Carnegie-Mellon School of Business (CMU) in Pittsburgh, Pennsylvania.

While finishing at CMU, Professor McGee attended a job fair at which the Research Division of Westinghouse in Pittsburgh (a separate Division) offered to pay for him to attend evening law school for four years at Duquesne University, if he worked at the Westinghouse Patent Department as a patent agent. As a patent agent, professor McGee wrote patent applications that were submitted to the United States Patent and Trademark Office (USPTO) for various Westinghouse inventions.

After graduating from Duquesne and interviewing with dozens of companies, Professor McGee accepted an offer in the Management Development Program at AT&T, where, in 4 years, he learned some valuable lessons in life and business. Soon after these lessons, he began his career in academia as described in brief above.

GEM 17

GEM 18

This I know for sure: *You must always be true to yourself and let your inner light shine.*

When I was ten years old, I was my true self and loved being that age. I wasn't afraid of my male counterparts and gleefully capsized their paper boats and airplanes when the need arose. I balanced on the tightrope of vulnerability and strength with ease. For me, nothing seemed impossible. My youth, my color, my gender, and my awareness of my sexual orientation bore me strength rather than weakness; they were my assets. I knew without question who I was and was unapologetic. I was a powerful and intelligent young black gay American girl with my entire life ahead of me, and I was happy.

My bubble burst soon, however. Slowly but surely, I began to lose the power of being self-assured and thereby let my inner light dim. It was through a process called "fitting in" that required me to relinquish my power.

My adolescent years were tumultuous. I didn't feel like I was being my authentic self and fell into despair and inner darkness. Though I tried to fit in and deny who I was, it just didn't work. My biology, hormones, and anatomy fought back and refused to let my inner light extinguish.

There is no denying that the desire to be loved and accepted by others is also a huge driver. Wanting to be myself but also needing to be accepted in the terms and conditions of others caused a major conflict that led me to prioritize the latter over the former. In making this choice, it was clear that what mattered most to me was that others loved me, not that I loved myself. It was debilitating. Looking back, I realize I was all too willing to compromise myself because I was afraid of not being loved. In the process, the power dynamic shifted upward, as I stepped down.

One day, I said, "no more." I looked into my heart and saw a cancer that I knew would only grow and I prayed for the strength to break out of the mold. I asked my 10-year-old self, "what matters to you most Shara Dae?" She answered, "the light." This reassured and redirected me and from then on, I listened to my inner voice and followed the path on which my inner light shined.

Once I was clarified and in alignment with my inner self, it was time to situate myself in the work world. I entered it as an openly gay black woman, which did not make it easy for me.

GEM 18

33 Gems ✦ Wisdom for Living Pieces of Life's Puzzle   77

Not only did I have to fight against discrimination on multiple levels, I also had to overcome the fact that I didn't have anyone to show me the way forward professionally.

At this point, I had to draw on a strength deep within me, my mother. She taught me how to adapt and make room for myself in a world that wasn't always kind or fair. Coming from a long line of resilient women, my mother has always been a force of nature. I know that my strength is a direct result of her brilliance. On difficult days in the office, I often found myself reaching back to memories of my childhood in order remember my mother's tenacity. The working mother, doing whatever it took to keep the lights on, she steadies me.

I had to carve my own road and pave my own way and I did it in the cut-throat heterosexual white male-dominated world of finance. While I was making it in this industry, it was making me something that I didn't want to be. In my heart, I knew the stock market wasn't my calling and as time went on, I increasingly felt this field wasn't in line with who I was at my core. I saw no purpose in making rich people wealthier.

So, I decided to regroup and redesign my life. My aim was to make a positive difference in the world, especially for the good of marginalized communities, but it wasn't clear how to do that.

I knew that in my next move, I wanted to use what I had learned about myself and the world to guide me in the right direction. I also knew that wherever I was going, I had to be my true self, just as I had been when I was 10 years old.

So, I went back to school to study journalism at the age of 35. I chose this field because I understood the power of media and of controlling how stories are told.

In my sophomore year, I managed to land my first internship with the top TV news station, WPVI-6abc. I was 36 years old. The other interns were 19 years old. Now, the battlefield changed; not only was I was of the few blacks and gay working at the station, the competition was coming from the rear guard of 19-year-old kids. Each day was a fight to get noticed and to build credibility. Unlike my younger competition, I also had to prove that I was not only capable and credible, but that my age wasn't a hinderance but rather was an advantage. Broadcasting, after all, is known for valuing youth and appearances over knowledge.

But here's the thing: With age comes wisdom and informed confidence. After 20 years in boardrooms in the finance world before I stepped a foot in the broadcasting room, I had learned many lessons, such as how to handle myself professionally in a work

GEM 18

environment and how to interpret news and not just report it. Fortunately, because I was recently attended university, I knew how to use both the latest computer editing software and the fax machine.

Most of the students had never seen a fax machine, nor had they heard of them. I, on the other hand, was raised on fax machines and on face-to face communication. These kids were raised on iPads and texting. In contrast to my younger cohort, I used both technology and interpersonal skills together, which was a distinct competitive advantage.

I don't know if the kids learned anything from me, but I sure learned a lot from them. They didn't play nicely in the sand box; what they lacked in knowledge, they made up for in their relentless drive to get ahead. I had to change my game as well and to be as hungry and driven. Every morning I had to "sell" my bosses on Shara Dae and what I was capable of and I had to help them to reinterpret the benefits of my being older than the rest.

I started winning. I beat out the others and was chosen to field produce a holiday story that played on 6ABC's "Good Morning America." I knew this was a turning point, but it would have been easy to become a "one trick pony." No, I had to stay on the case and constantly create demand for my talents.

At this point I was still in school. In the next class I took, my professor arranged a walk through at the KYW-CBS3 TV station. Ah ha, "this was my chance." I printed up business cards and during the walk through, I walked right on over to the News Director's office and introduced myself. The night before, I had done my homework and learned everything about her career. She was a formidable woman with a respected name in journalism. Though she was notorious for being "too busy" to talk to anyone, she wound up talking with me for over 20 minutes. When I got up to leave I thanked her for her time and said: "I may be older, but I'm bolder and I handed her my card. She was visibly impressed.

She emailed me the next day and the Assistant News Director called me in for an interview the next week.

At age 37, I was offered a job at both WPVI-6abc and KYW-CBS3, two of the leading broadcast stations in Philadelphia. It happened because I created demand for me!

I took the job as a news assistant at CBS3 and started out answering phones and quickly began assignment editing and producing special projects. The wide range of exposure to broadcasting at such a high level enabled me to quickly glean where I fit in. Knowing who I was at the core helped me to discern this. I didn't just want to fit their team, I wanted their team to fit me.

GEM 18

I spent 3.5 years with CBS3. While there, I developed a solid network and many important contacts. These would be critical for my next career in radio.

It turns out the TV business was on a downturn, losing money each year. Layoffs became the norm at our TV station while radio and webcasting were on the rise. Reading the writing on the wall, I took a deep breath, regrouped again, and readied myself to transition over to radio.

To get my feet in this door, I had to do what I had always done: "Sell myself." This time, however, I had a network of colleagues to draw on. Today, I am the Editing Producer and Reporter for one of the largest radio news companies in the nation. In this endeavor, and throughout my life, I remain true to myself.

My goal is to create my own brand and network station one day. No one showed me the way, but I want to show others what I have learned, especially marginalized populations, and let my light illuminate their pathways to success.

✦ ✦ ✦

Gem 18 Essayist: **Shara Dae Howard**

Ms. Howard is a TV and Radio journalist, editor and broadcast reporter. After 20 successful years in the financial industry, she worked her way to up to the position of Associate VP of Business and Development at a one of the most respected wealth management firms in Philadelphia. After 20 years in the financial business, she pivoted and made a significant life change. Wanting to serve her community best, Ms. Howard decided to transition from finance to journalism. To do so, she went back to university and graduated from Temple University with a B.A. in Broadcast Journalism, with a focus on globalism and development. Directly out of school, she field produced for WRTI-6abc and KYW-CBS3, two of the top TV News stations in Philadelphia, before becoming a News Editor and Reporter at KYW News radio. As a news editor and reporter, she interviews high profile community members and neighbors alike, helping to share their stories with the world. As a Journalist, Ms. Howard is working toward being the voice for those who remain unheard in marginalized communities all over our country and the world.

GEM 19

This I know for sure:
If you want to thrive in life and over its long haul, you must design yourself to do that!

I am 77 years old and am an ultra-marathon runner, which means I run distances over 26.2 miles. Note that I said I "am" an ultra-marathon runner, not that I "was" one. I designed myself to do that.

Such a design happens through a process over many decades that entails making many lifestyle changes. I started when I was 29 years old.

At that age, I weighed over 200 pounds, was sedentary, and smoked cigarettes, and I had a three-year-old daughter. One day, she wanted to play tag. She tagged me and said, "I bet you can't catch me!" I couldn't catch her, or my breath. It was a "wake up call."

I knew I had to do something, but I didn't know where to start. Naturally, I thought about going on a diet because that's what people did then; that's all we knew about.

I discovered Dr. Gabe Mirkin's radio show. He would talk about health, fitness, and nutrition. He made complete sense to me! I'd listen to him every day while I was preparing dinner and I started making small changes. I didn't know his message was sinking in, but gradually I started focusing on what I was eating and preparing for my family, then I began to think about the need to engage in physical movement.

Though I was internalizing and acting upon his wisdom, which became my foundation for change, I wanted to take another step, one that took me closer to nature because nature had always been my trusted playmate and best friend when I was growing up. I remember that I loved playing in the woods and fell in love with dandelions and their story. Many people think of dandelions as weeds and have done everything to try to get rid of them, but they survived and even thrived. I wanted to be "dandelion-like."

I found that I was seeking a life solution that had the features of resiliency just like those of a dandelion. I observed that resiliency had two main properties: **patience** and **simplicity**. Therefore, I knew that being healthy meant going beyond just losing weight; I had to change my entire lifestyle incrementally, over a period of time.

GEM 19

I had only one option for doing this: I had to re-design myself. My redesign was all-encompassing and required me to bring forth nature's wisdom that was already in me.

Reflecting on the properties of nature, I further realized that there were two main keys to becoming healthy: **nutrition** and **fitness**. In changing the former, my goal was to try to eat things in a manner that was closest to how nature provided them (so instead of eating blueberry pie; I just ate the blueberries). The same holds true in the realm of fitness; to try to move in a way that the body was designed to move. For instance, the body is designed to use gravity to propel itself forward, rather than relying solely on muscles. Movement that runs contrary to nature is bound to cause injury.

On my journey of change, I began by walking for two minutes each day, then gradually got up to running 2 miles a day, every day. This didn't happen overnight; getting to 2 miles took about eight months. Eventually, I moved up to running, in about one year.

Looking back, I reckon that I took six major steps to re-design myself. The first step was harnessing my internal strength. The second step was entailed making my mind and body agreeable allies. The third step entailed bringing together my nutrition and movement into an actionable program of activities. The fourth step called for stepping across the lifestyle change line. The fifth step entailed seeking and taking on new nutrition and fitness challenges, and the sixth step was— and is—the need to constantly recalibrate my program for my age to ensure that I am **aging agelessly**.

I ran my first marathon in 1988 – The Marine Corps Marathon. My second marathon was the Moscow International Peace Marathon. Since that time, I have run 79 more marathons throughout the world, and have run 25 ultra-marathons since 2007. **Today, I run marathons in order to train for ultra-marathons.**

I have a 3-hour routine in the morning that consists of strengthening, flexibility, balance and relaxation exercises: then I finish up with T'ai Chi, and meditation. I'm then in a different state of mind, ready to take on whatever the day has in store.

I run 24, 48, 72 and 144-hour (6-day) events and people want to know how? But people don't want to hear about my hour workout routine (before I run), but they want your outcomes. I run 60 to 100 miles a week depending on when the next ultra-marathon will be held. Presently, I am preparing to enter a 10-day race in which I will run 10 days and 10 nights on minimal sleep.

I can run night and day because my energy recreates itself rather than depleting itself. Therefore, I have more energy at the end of these races than at the beginning.

GEM 19

Johns Hopkins's Bloomberg School of Public Health is following my progress and is interested in my energy levels as I age.

My physicians are amazed: I am carefully monitored by them. They say I am at least 20 years younger than my chronological age. My blood, bones, heart - are all healthy. When my cardiologist listened to my heart, he was saying "wow", not with concern, but with amazement about how efficient my heart is. (Resting rate of 28-30 beats per minute).

Basically, I took nature up on its offer to live according to "dandelion principles". If you do the same, you will have everything you will need to re-design yourself and to age agelessly. I give nature the credit for my accomplishments. My re-design step-by-step process is featured in my upcoming autobiographical sketch, *"Lifestyle by Nature."* It is scheduled to reach book shelves and on-line by the summer of 2018, Author House, publisher.

✦ ✦ ✦

Gem 19 Essayist: **Betty H. Smith, Ed.D.**

Dr. Betty Smith is a minimal shoe/barefoot ultra-marathon runner. She has run on all 7 Continents and completed nearly 100 marathons and ultra-marathons combined. A runner for 43 years, she is an age-group nationally ranked ultra-marathoner and has set national age-group records in the 48 hours and 6-day road races under USA-Track and Field guidelines. She has only had one significant running injury which happened more than 15 years ago, out of a total of over 100,000 miles. Dr. Betty has run about 60 weekly ultra-marathon training miles for over 6 years without injury or need for recovery. She is a RRCA and USATF certified coach who *obviously* follows her own coaching advice. In addition to holding an Ed.D., she also holds a Master's in Business and Public Administration.

GEM 19

GEM 20

This I know for sure:

For many Americans diagnosed with a serious illness such as cancer, navigating a path to wellness through our fragmented health care system can be daunting, fraught with missteps and unclear directions. To achieve best possible outcomes, they must learn to engage in their care as informed patients, often with an advocate—whether a family member or a professional—at their side.

In many cases these days, the burden has fallen to patients to map their own way through our complex health care landscape. It's a domain with unique language, highways and byways, and timetables. What is an already stressful experience can become overwhelming and many people start to feel lost. To make the system work for them, patients need to engage in this new world, to step up as confident, informed, and equal partners in their care—but many lack the tools, knowledge and or experience to do so.

This is where I come in as a patient coach and advocate, to help fill the gap in tools, knowledge, and experience in health care system navigation. Patient coaching and advocacy was a shadow career for most of my life—one that grew out of demand from a network of friends. On a mid-career return to my native California, I chose to embrace patient advocacy on a full-time basis and my business has grown to include clients nationwide and overseas. I help them develop coordinated action plans for care, including identifying the medical and complementary resources best suited to them and their lifestyle, priorities, and medical profile. My goal is to give them the tools they need to advocate for themselves and to help them access clinically valid, scientific advances in their areas of medical need. The old "one size fits all" model of medicine doesn't work and is being transformed by providing more precise and personalized care.

My interests in patient advocacy began with my mother's illness in the late 1960s—it was the "dark ages" of managing aggressive breast cancer. Mom spent considerable time in the hospital (one of the nations most renowned) and in recovering from multiple surgeries and the intensive therapies that doctors threw at her. She was "game" for everything. Despite all efforts, she died five years after being diagnosed—she was just 44 years old.

GEM 20

Through her cancer journey, I witnessed firsthand some of the dehumanizing and debilitating experiences that patients endure. Experiences that were unnecessarily severe in terms of a patient's agency, and certainly, in terms of their dignity. After one surgery, my mother told me that the only kind people at the hospital had been the "Candy Stripers"—everyone else had been treating the disease, not caring for the person. She felt dismissed and unheard. This was wholly unlike my mother to complain about anything—she was incredibly stoic, strong, courageous and protective of her family. Surely, there was need for change in cancer care.

A few years after my mother died, one of my best friends—age 24—was also diagnosed with breast cancer. I applied all the knowledge I had gained from those years at the hospital with mom and used it to help "Sue" navigate her way through the doctors, labs, surgery and treatments. I cooked healthy meals for her and did "mind-body" work with her. In many respects, she became my first "client" as a patient coach. We avoided some missteps; but others occurred. Again, there were too many instances of doctors and nurses treating the disease, but not the whole person. Sadly, "Sue's" cancer spread like wildfire and she died 18 months from date of her initial diagnosis. These two experiences launched a lifetime commitment to aiding those in need of support as they navigated their cancer journeys.

Health care delivery has changed significantly since my mother's illness—gone are the days when a patient can treat a doctor's visit like taking the car to the mechanic, saying: "Say, doc, she's making some funny noises under the hood—could you have a look, maybe do a tune up, and I'll be back to pick her up later." Now, we have a fragmented and complex system of care—it is folly to abdicate one's own personal responsibility in achieving wellness. Patients must be active and involved. Again, this is where I come in: coaching clients on becoming equal partners in their care, as responsible, engaged and knowledgeable patients who can self-advocate as needed. When they show up in this manner, doctors are more inclined to treat them as equal partners. Patients are, after all, the only expert on the planet in themselves. The doctor is the expert in the human body. Together, as partners, they can identify and implement the right decisions.

My success in patient coaching and advocacy is based in my academic training in systems-based thinking, scientific research, and communications. I also bring compassion and caring, and take the time to listen deeply to a client's narrative—picking up elements that may be lost in the rush of the typical doctor's appointment. My approach entails assembling longitudinal data from diverse sources; tailoring tools to help the client achieve their goals; researching state-of-the art for their disease; and

GEM 20

tapping into my network of medical professionals to find the right match of providers, services and complementary care.

Here are two examples of how clients benefit from coaching. "Bob" came to me with a melanoma cancer diagnosis. He had no idea where to start in his search for the right surgeon and, if needed, the right oncologist. His dermatologist sent him to a general surgeon who had little experience with scalp melanomas; that doctor referred him to a head and neck surgeon who was a very nice person, but it became clear that he had not kept up with practice updates. Finally, based on my research, "Bob" made an appointment with one of the top head and neck surgeons in the West—whom he enthusiastically then chose as his surgeon. There were numerous twists and turns involving insurance and other issues—but with coaching, "Bob" did an excellent job of negotiating and navigating his way to the surgical suite, knowing that he was getting the most advanced care available. Had he stayed with the second doctor, he might have experienced long term repercussions such as lymphedema, and might not have had access to the advanced treatments now considered standard of care. Happily, his nodes were clear and surgery was curative. My client is over the moon with the outcome—and now has a new dermatologist.

Another client, diagnosed with a highly elevated PSA count (a protein produced in the prostate gland) and prostate cancer, had a Midwestern doctor who was eager to treat him with external beam radiation therapy—which for many men can lead to significant adverse effects in terms of urological and sexual health. A second doctor in Florida, known nationwide for his prostate cancer practice, recommended (via a telephone consult) an even more intensive approach. My client was very leery. I identified an outstanding specialist at Mayo Clinic in Minnesota for a third opinion.

Upon physical exam, the doctor stated that based on his years of experience in a high volume center, this prostate cancer was not as aggressive as the PSA numbers might suggest. He recommended a more conservative approach, putting put my client on hormone therapy and then bringing him back to Mayo eight months later for radioactive seed implants. His check-ups to date are great and my client is thrilled. This treatment was less intense, less invasive, and has fewer adverse effects. Bottom line: you cannot do medicine by "numbers" alone (one size does not fit all); there is no substitute for an excellent physical exam and a doctor who sees hundreds of cases each year.

I see the results of what happens when clients abdicate self-advocacy, especially with aging patients. One 75-year old client, under treatment for hypertension, did not realize that she had developed a frequent comorbid condition: kidney disease. Her doctor had not told her that her kidney function had dropped by 30% in 9 months and was well below the minimum threshold. But she had also not been checking her test results. With coaching, she learned about the hazards of kidney disease and demanded to see a nephrologist; this specialist told her that her kidney would be fine for a while, then would decline to the point at which dialysis would normally be considered. However, he stated: ... "patients in your age group don't do so well with dialysis—so I will refer you to hospice instead." Stunned silence. I coached my client on obtaining a second opinion with someone in whom I had more confidence. Wholly different story: Yes, said the second nephrologist, these kidney numbers CAN be reversed if my client adopted a vegan diet and cut back on her smoking. Sure enough: eight weeks later her kidney function numbers were soaring back towards normal. Without bringing in a patient coach, this 75-year old had been on a clear path to kidney failure and death—not even knowing that this was her fate. Now, she reviews her lab results with regular visits to the new doctor, and speaks up to get the health care she deserves.

We have a health care system that for all of its tech wonders and research advances, does not always meet the medical needs of many Americans. This I know for sure: Patients can achieve better health, if they are willing to invest in themselves with good care and nutrition, reliable research and information, a willingness to engage in partnership with their doctors, and an ability to self-advocate to get the help that they need. If they cannot achieve this on their own—especially as they get started—they should consider consulting with a professional patient coach or advocate. So doing will serve them throughout their medical journey and empower them to engage more effectively in their health care as informed advocates.

✦ ✦ ✦

GEM 20

Gem 20 Essayist: **CJ Hunter**

CJ Hunter is an expert patient coach and health care navigator who guides clients as they navigate the health care system towards best possible health outcomes. With her help, clients learn to tackle difficult health care challenges with confidence and authority. CJ works with them to develop a comprehensive roadmap to care that integrates personal, work and health priorities. CJ translates the basics of relevant medical science, and helps clients build their health literacy and skills. She identifies possible clinical trials and clinically-valid translational science, as well as evidence-based complementary treatments, for consideration with their doctor. When needed, CJ collects and organizes a client's medical data that she distills for "at a glance" understanding of their health status and trends. CJ brings a wealth of expertise to patient coaching from her years working in science policy issues in Congress and at the White House, as the CEO of several businesses (from manufacturing to sustainability), as a leader in promoting sustainability, and as a lifelong patient coach. She holds graduate degrees from MIT in science policy and business.

For further information, please visit: *www.apatientcoach.com.*

GEM 21

This I know for sure:
Each of us has the opportunity to improve on our parents' influence, if we can only muster the tremendous courage and insight it takes to do so.

I was born to two damaged people.

My mother only reluctantly tells the stories of her father beating her and her brother, going beyond the line between discipline and abuse. Her father berated them both, bruised them, and disowned them several times. Her mother would often come to them after the abuse had taken place, and try to soothe and comfort them, saying "Shhh… It's okay… You'll be all right…" However, this soothing and comforting rang hollow, in the context of her mother's complicity in the abuse while it was happening. One time, in the evening before her brother was to be sent to Vietnam, her father raised his glass and presented the following toast: "Here's hoping those 'gooks' get ya." This was the household in which my mother had to grow up, fending for herself and learning about life in between and through the dark times.

My father, now deceased, was born to an alcoholic father. There was similar abuse on his side as well; my father told me once that as a punishment for some mistake he had made, his father made him sit down and watch him put a gun to his mother's head and pull the trigger. The gun wasn't loaded, so his mother lived, but my father's inner life was slowly being ravaged by the collection of horror stories he was experiencing. It took some time for all this trauma to wreak its inevitable havoc on my father's psyche and when he was laid off from his job, the stress and perceived insult to his masculinity pitched him down into a chronic depression that never lifted.

And yet, and yet, despite the abusive parenting in their backgrounds, my parents did not abuse their own children. My brother and I received our fair share of spankings, but I am certain that there were limits to the number of hits and amount of force that was used. Sure, there were times when my parents (my father in particular) spoke to me in harsh tones and with unkind words, but I never felt as if I wasn't wanted; they never left marks on me, or toasted my death, or pulled any guns on me.

The more writing and reflection I engage in about what psychologists call the "intergenerational transmission of parenting practices," the more I admire my parents'

GEM 21

ability to treat my brother and me differently to how they had been treated. The research into people who come from my parents' type of background is consistent – most people parent their children in the same way that they were treated when they were children. Abuse victims tend to abuse their own children, and parents who were made to feel small and worthless when they were children carry that legacy into their own parenting, unless there is a level of self-awareness and righteous anger about the past.

My parents both knew that they had been abused, and they also knew that the abuse they had experienced had damaged them at a deep psychological level. And yet, they made a decision, in spite of the powerful gravitational pull of the past, to stop the cycle from continuing.

It's been my mission to continue the good work they began with me. My father's depression began when I was nine years old and my brother three. His breakdown was swift and came down like a sledgehammer on a glass nail. While I am grateful for the lighter form of corporal punishment that he used as a consequence, and my mother's attempts to smooth things over with compliments, my childhood wasn't perfect by any means.

After my father was laid off and he became too disabled to find any other employment, we sank into poverty – Section 8 housing, food stamps, SSI... My father stayed in bed most days, staring up at the ceiling, rising only to eat, and smoke cigarettes in the bathroom. He didn't take me out to throw ball, or ask me much about my day, or show very much interest in me at all. My mother, devastated by the loss of her husband, sank into her own form of depression, feeding the void with ever larger amounts of food. Eventually, something had to be done about our finances, and my mother decided to go to college. She graduated and got a job as a teacher, accomplishing this amazing feat just before my father's death. All this meant that for a good chunk of my adolescence, I was alone while my father stared catatonically into space, and my mother tried to muster the energy to keep us all afloat.

When I had my own children, lacking a "normal" model, in many ways it was up to me to try to figure out what good parents looked like. All my life, I've had to perform this kind of masquerading. When I needed to learn how to be self-confident, I observed self-confident people and then mimicked them – how they held themselves, how they dressed, and their vocabulary. And, when I wanted to have more friends, I looked around at the popular kids and noted anything they did that might help me to achieve my goal. My method had been to look for models of success and copy them, and

GEM 21

now, it was up to me to learn about parenting. Luckily, however, by the time I was a daddy, I was also a research psychologist, and so had access to libraries of research on positive parenting practices.

This is what seems to be the key to successfully parenting children who function well in the world: *Be kind to them.* They are, after all, human beings and as such, they should be treated the way human beings deserve (and would like) to be treated. It goes even further than that: they are human beings who are soaking up every little bit of information they can, trying hard to make sense of a world into which they have been inexplicably flung. As Peggy O'Mara once said, "The way you speak to your child becomes his/her inner voice." I'd extend that further and say that the way you treat your child will become the way he treats himself when he is older.

Once I began to realize that what children need more than anything is to feel loved, valued, and worthwhile, I had a rule of thumb to guide my fathering and if anything was inconsistent with this rule of thumb, then it had to go. Spankings, ridicule, insults? None of these made any sense to me as part of a plan to create successful human beings who would make decisions based on a belief in their own preciousness. It's my job to help my children believe, and this means making time in my schedule to talk to them about their interests, ask them questions, prioritize them, play with them, and give them kind advice. I was eager to be the best parent I could be.

You, reader, have the same capacity to think about the lives of your children, and decide to parent them in a way that is consistent with your philosophy, responsive to your history, and convinced of your power to build a new way. Somewhere in your family's history, someone needs to improve the script. Why can't it be you? Have courage; the past has already happened, but the future is yours to create.

◆ ◆ ◆

GEM 21

Gem 21 Essayist: John Rich, Ph.D.

Dr. John D Rich, Jr. is an educational psychologist, former United Methodist minister, and associate professor of Psychology at Delaware State University, with expertise in effective parenting and teaching. He is also the proud father of two boys, Josiah and Jesse, and the lucky husband of Erin Rich.

Dr. Rich believes that most people desire to live a happy, ethical life. He also believes that we can come closer to achieving that desire when we think intentionally and consciously about the decisions that our lives present to us. Through such intentionality, engaging in conversation and reflection, we can become better people, and build a better society.

Dr. Rich writes about parenting and teaching on his website. In addition, his writing appears on esteemed websites like the ones for Psychology Today, the American Psychological Association, the Good Men Project, Edutopia (funded by the George Lucas Foundation) and a news site in New Hampshire. He also has a radio show called "Dr John's Neighborhood.

Dr. Rich is looking forward to the upcoming release of his first book on parenting, which will be released this Spring. In addition to the places where his online writing has appeared, he has been published in over 40 different academic journals on topics related to teaching and parenting.

Dr. Rich is currently broadening his work to include counseling with parents, in one-on-one and group (online) settings. If you or someone you know is experiencing parenting challenges that require attention or support.

GEM 21

GEM 22

This I know for sure:
Resilience is seated in the depth of our connections to ourselves and to others.

To survive and to thrive we can't be disconnected from any part of ourselves or from major parts of our tribe. We are communal by nature and bounce back better from adversity when we know who we are at our core and when we are willing to share those truths with others who positively influence us. We are more likely to reach our potential for greatness when we know ourselves well, connect deeply with those who support us, and use life lessons as fuel to keep things moving.

I grew up with a hard-working single parent who, no matter the circumstances, always found a way to put one foot in front of the other to keep things going. It didn't matter what the difficulty was – financial, emotional, relational, spiritual, or intellectual, she moved forward. Not only did she keep going in a positive direction, she did so with four children in tow. Over time, acute issues were resolved. In the end, she was always seen as a loving and forgiving being who was able to walk proudly with confidence and liberation.

As the oldest girl, I was always on the front lines of helping to resolve family issues. From my lens, success was gained by standing strong and continuing no matter what. As I saw it, mom could do anything and overcome everything, and she was training me to be just like her. She was teaching me how to dig deep and let the event create the elasticity I needed to move on, move out, and move up. She was showing me how to move on by releasing that which doesn't serve me; to move out by executing mission; and to move up by elevating the importance of whatever role I was in while remaining connected to my inner and outer circles. She was giving me the tools to become resilient.

As I ran into challenges as a pre-teen and teenager, she would use our special code word in addressing me and would say: "Chevrolet!" That meant keep moving forward, one foot after another. Over time, I gained a deeper understanding and realized she meant that some things were conquered by sheer brute force while others were achieved with grace. "Chevrolet" was an order to be introspective, gather my greatest intentions and ideas, and use them to resolve difficulties.

GEM 22

In the 1980s, I entered the workforce armed with resilience. At a time when Reaganomics was the fiduciary driver, the Berlin Wall was solid, and Apartheid was gaining global interest, I became a police officer in a large southern city. I soon realized that I had moved to a place where remnants of all of those things converged; a place where racial tensions and gang violence co-existed with concrete cowboys who had confederate blood running through their veins. While the cowboys knew that the Civil War had ended, they believed the south had won. The young, impressionable, and resilient me donned the blue and moved out quickly. In my first full-time paying job, notwithstanding the turbulence of injustice and inequality, I made a name for myself as someone who could dig deep, plod through the minefield, and make it to the other shore alive with my blue troop by my side.

Two years and eleven police funerals later, I moved on by releasing the blue uniform and all the notoriety came with it while keeping the lessons the experience gave me. I moved from the confines of a city and a uniform to covertly enforcing the laws nationally and later internationally. Over the next 17 years, and through each international incident, political crisis, national disaster, human tragedy, and personal misfortune, my resilience led to individual successes that built upon one another, layer by layer. Whether it was the stand-off at Ruby Ridge, the riots in Los Angeles, the siege at Waco, the bombing in Oklahoma City, the events of 9/11, Operation Desert Storm, Operation Inherent Resolve, entry into single motherhood, or the impacts of transitions of life of friends and family, I learned more about myself and strengthened my connection with my tribe. In each assignment, job, and role, I became better at using both a jack hammer and a feather to move forward; sometimes with force and other times with finesse.

In the last ten years, to deepen my introspection, dial back the intensity, find balance, and to shine lights on the bright spots of my life's journey, I started practicing yoga and meditation. Although I had a reputation for being the person who can solve most problems, it was yoga and meditation that stretched me to my outer edges. By combining the lessons from my mom with the new teachings from meditation, moving through challenges became a smoother process. Equally, my relationships with members of my tribe became much more like a tapestry that illustrates the calming effects of the intricacies of life – the beauty of the simplicities and the fascination with the complexities encountered in the journey.

The lessons from my mom were the seedlings and slow nurturing of what I learned and now live through yoga and meditation. Through them, I have learned that like a tree, your tribe is an extension of you or branches from your trunk. Some are stronger,

GEM 22

and some are longer. Some are stiff while most are flexible and able to bend with the changing of the wind whirling around. These trees can weather many storms and changes of seasons. They survive and then thrive during pruning, with leaves growing and then falling as they die. They never lose their identity as a tree or their connection from their roots. They always remain grounded while bending without breaking; always forgiving the wind for its turbulence and loving nature as it is. Most importantly, their roots carry the DNA of everything that is planted around them, just as we carry the memories and life lessons of those around us.

As I retire and move into my next chapter in life, I will continue to rely on lessons from my mom as a reminder of how to make it around obstacles and through the unknown. Yoga and meditation are also guides to help with the push and pull of life that stretches and grows me with grace. Likewise, I ask that you too look, listen, and learn from the people and events that enter your path. Whether it is the remembrance of your special "Chevrolet" code word or some other lesson from a guru in your life, each has the power to teach, expand, and help you evolve towards your potential for greatness.

✦ ✦ ✦

Gem 22 Essayist: **Lisa McClennon**

Ms. McClennon is a seasoned global enforcement and compliance executive who specializes in investigations and integrated enterprise risk management. She began her career in law enforcement in 1987 as a Reserve Police Officer serving the public's interests by enforcing city ordinances and regulations. Later, she became a full time commissioned Police Officer. By 1991, she began her work as a federal agent on tiger teams, identifying and prosecuting disreputable gun dealers and odious buyers who were selling guns that ended up in poor underserved neighborhoods.

She transferred to the Immigration and Naturalization Service where she sanctioned employers by levying fines against them when they exploited undocumented workers with less than fair labor wages. In 1999, at the U.S. Department of housing and Urban Development – Office of Inspector General, she joined cross functional teams that prosecuted defendants who preyed on uneducated and desperate populations. The

GEM 22

defendants paid the under-resourced people to become straw buyers in mortgage fraud at loan origination schemes that that contributed to homelessness and led to foreclosures of thousands of homes, further decimating poor and deteriorating neighborhoods of color. From 2002 to 2018, she used her highly honed investigative skills globally at the US Agency for International Development – Office of Inspector General leading international investigative teams. She holds a B.S. in Criminal Justice from Texas State University; a M.S. in Human Relations and Business from Amberton University; and has done post-graduate work in Urban Policy and Administration from the University of Texas at Arlington. She has also obtain certificates in ethics, compliance, and leadership. She currently serves as a consultant on leadership with the International Association of Chiefs of Police.

GEM 22

GEM 23

This I know for sure:
I was born in a New York City hospital in 1952, yet the essence of me was began long before that year.

I was born the third and last child of Jack and Rachel Robinson. I am male. I am of the African American tribe, and a member of the family of mankind. I am the child of many, many generations. I am not a learned historian, but I acknowledge and embrace my family's position within the human history of the last 10,000 years. I am of the blood, memory, and essence of all these past generations. I am born with the desire to live, to support life and work towards conditions that will sustain life for future generations. While my largest self-image is as a member of humanity, my work focus is family, tribe, and race. I believe we humans were created and developed with differences and that the strengthening of positive human evolution will require the sub-sets of humanity to enhance their individual contributions to the whole.

My parentage and the social climate of my youth greatly helped to illuminate the true situation and dynamics faced by African Americans. Bull Connor, George Wallace, and Richard Nixon were part of the vocal and "would-be" powerful leadership firmly set against the inclusion and ascension of African Americans. We met them in mass. Students, ordinary workers, clergy, and housewives marched on the front-lines of opposition. Our organizations from the NAACP to the Black Panthers gave clarity to our different analyses and operational plans.

I was 15 when my parents showed me our African homeland in Ghana, Kenya, Ethiopia, and Tanzania. I was 18 when I took up rocks and bottles in the fury of indignation. I was 19 when I returned to Africa to continue identity exploration rather than complete my university degree at Stanford University.

My parents and victories in social challenge told me definitively of our capacity and opportunity. Assassination, conspiracy, domestic and foreign wars, drugs and death radicalized me in the faces of subjugation reorganized. As my thoughts evolved the voices of family past spoke invisibly from the huge corridors of time: "We were, we are, we endured, we will be. One day, little brother, one day"

And so, I returned to America from Tanzania in 1971. Employed by my father's real estate development company, I loved the physical labor of construction. After his death in 1972, my associations within the Harlem community and political organizations

GEM 23

lead a group of us to study the potentials and opportunities in Harlem's structural redevelopment. From Harlem's physical chaos and decay a picture of a giant field of uncut diamonds to be mined and polished formed clearly within our understanding. We incorporated under the name "United Harlem Growth, Inc." We rallied, organized, and bullied support from the expanding rings of community control beginning with the 136 street Block Association; The St. Nicholas Community Council; the Harlem Planning Boards; and extending downtown to the federal Housing and Urban Development Corporation; and the seeming foreign country of New York's City Hall. We acquired "Official Developer" status for 16 Harlem Brownstones. In Phase One, we purchased and secured title for 5 buildings at $500 each.

These were the "going rates" negotiable in the 1970s when Harlem had reached its peak of exploitation, neglect, abandonment, and ultimate City ownership via tax foreclosures. Under "United Harlem Growth's" intellectual concepts, "City owned" meant "Community owned". Under the operational plan of cooperative "Sweat Equity" with the support of the Block Association only, we began extensive demolition and construction preparation with our own labor and financing. This work was done nine months before obtaining any official City government recognition.

Over a 5-year struggle, United Harlem Growth obtained bank financing and federal mortgages at 3% for 20 years. We completed construction and "Sweet Equity" families occupied the five brownstones.

Our success in large part was due to the intense commitment to self-help embraced by the working class founding families and the unique sustaining bonds within the core leadership.

However, we failed in the longer term to build unity from within the diversity of the African American community. The first families succeeded with heart and determination, but organizational sustainability would require levels of education, skills, and an operational sophistication that existed within another segment of the African American community. We, the founders, did not have the ability to convince that segment to join and manage our Phase Two Sweat Equity undertaking. By 1982, I had turned down opportunities to work within the traditional development construction industry and was set on a course to return to Africa. United Harlem Growth Inc. was headed towards fatigue and collapse.

As I write today, I am in Tanzania; my home for the last 35 years. Eight of my 10 children were born on the African continent. In 1989, my family and neighbors began to clear forest and establish a farm we called "Sweet Unity". We grow coffee and food

GEM 23

crops. We are founders and part of a cooperative of family-owned farms and export coffee to North America. We roast and sell this coffee under the brand name "Sweet Unity Farms" *www.sweetunityfarmscoffee.com*.

Our work focuses on the utilization of global African resources towards self-help, survival and development. Childhood opportunities and experience has led me into a global positioning. We people of the African race live on many continents. We are internationally wealthy in resources both human and natural. As we export, import, process and sell coffee, we work with peoples of different races and religions. We work as part of the family of man.

This I know for sure; only the smallest, least significant part of me was born in 1952. I love my 10,000-year-old family who are the essence of me and my children who are the essence of us. I know also that I cannot know all things, hence I believe and have faith. Humanity is and has been engaged in bitter struggle. The suffering is horrendous. Yet we are, I believe, created with the potential to build harmony and sustain life. I believe our ancestors and our unborn children call on the living, to struggle for the fulfillment of this human potential.

✦ ✦ ✦

Gem 23 Essayist: **David Robinson**

David Robinson was born in 1952 as the youngest child of legendary Jackie Robinson and his wife Rachel. Growing up during the African-American Civil Rights Movement of the 1960s, and in the Robinson home where such issues were at the core of everyday life, David Robinson has spent the last 40 years involved in the development of racial and human opportunity. David serves on the board of the Jackie Robinson Foundation — an organization that his mother, Rachel Robinson, founded in 1973 as a vehicle to perpetuate the memory of Jackie Robinson and his achievements.

Since 1983, David has been involved in the economic development of Africa through sustainable agriculture. David is the founder and managing director of Higher Ground Development, an organization that works directly with coffee cooperatives. In 1998, David also founded Up-Country International Products Inc., the sole distributor and

GEM 23

marketer of **Sweet Unity Farms Coffee**. *(www.sweetunityfarmscoffee.com/pages/mission*. The mission of Sweet Unity Farms is to enhance the economic position and quality of life for rural coffee farmers and their communities. Through direct trade partnerships with coffee roasters and marketing companies, the creation of branded coffee products and a system of equitable income distribution, Sweet Unity Farms Coffee strives to be part of a successful business model for global citizenship wherein international economic growth and human development move forward together.

David is the father of ten children, and resides in Tanzania with his wife and younger children. He and his family spend their time between the coffee farm in Mbeya and their home in the coastal city of Dar es Salaam. David's story has recently been featured on ESPN in a film by Spike Lee: *(http://www.espn.com/video/clip?id=13341605)*

GEM 23

GEM 24

This I know for sure:
As you travel on life's highway, it's important to serve and help others, and not just yourself.

I truly believe that the more you give, the more you will receive. This is the philosophy I've espoused all of my life, and especially during my 41-year career in the U.S. Foreign Service (FS).

It was my destiny to be in the Foreign Service because I have been "in service" all my life, one way or another.

My mother, now 96 years old, showed me how to and the necessity of serving others. She reared nine children on her own after my father passed away at the young age of 39, living on my father's meager pension of $18 per child monthly, which she supplemented with earnings from domestic and field work in rural Edgecombe, N.C. A proud woman, she refused to accept public assistance and instead, my siblings and I were pressed into service at early ages. We worked the family's 12 rows of tobacco, picked blueberries, cotton, and did other farm chores. Being the third oldest, when I was eleven, in addition to working in the fields, I helped by cleaning hotel rooms, washing dishes in restaurants, and scrubbing church floors to add to the household income.

It's a miracle that many years later, I reached the rank of Ambassador in the Foreign Service. It was a hard, uphill climb from being educated in substandard segregated schools for the first six grades in a one-teacher school to being bused on a 34-mile roundtrip each day to attend elementary and high school.

Who would have imagined that from such a background, I would be plucked from obscurity, starting when in high school, I was voted the "Female Most Likely to Succeed." This honor led to a scholarship to attend North Carolina College, from which I graduated with a B.Sc. in Business Education. It was providence that I joined the Alpha Kappa Alpha, Sorority, Inc. (AKA), whose motto is "Service to all Mankind."

For me, being in "Service to all Mankind" is not just a motto; it is the way I have lived my life. Because of my belief in serving others, I applied to join the U.S. Peace Corps, and was accepted and assigned to Sierra Leone in West Africa. My mother intervened, however; she didn't want me to go so I could stay home and continue to help with the family and my siblings, and I obliged.

GEM 24

Later, I accepted employment at the U.S. Department of Agriculture (USDA) as a low-level secretary, despite my college education. It was unfair, given my education, that I had to begin my government career on the lowest rung of the ladder, but the reality is that in the mid-1960s, African American college graduates were simply not hired for jobs in their area of study, or given salaries that were commensurate with the positions and salaries given to white college graduates.

Job title and salary notwithstanding, it was no "day at the park" working at USDA. There was no "bench" of other African Americans there to mentor or guide me in how to flourish, and all I had to rely on was my survival instinct. To survive, I had to become the captain and crew of my own ship and navigate in treacherous waters to find and seize opportunities. One such great opportunity was USDA's Foreign Agricultural Service (FAS). Upon discovering the FAS, I realized that it presented a potential avenue for me to work abroad one day.

My heart lay in working overseas, but I had to "work" the system to get there, so I learned French, which was the key for obtaining a temporary assignment as a secretary in the U.S. Mission in Geneva, Switzerland. Speaking French also led to me being assigned to a four-year assignment as a secretary in the Office of Agricultural Affairs at the U.S. Mission to the Organization for Economic Cooperation and Development (USOECD) in Paris, France.

I realized that if I were to ever climb higher than the secretarial level, I had to obtain a graduate degree, so I took a leave of absence and completed an M.Sc. Degree in Business Administration and Economics at North Carolina Central University. When I returned to the FAS, I expected to be placed in a much higher professional position but even with a graduate degree, it wasn't easy or automatic to move up.

I kept plugging away and took courses in agricultural economics, research, and international trade at the USDA Graduate School, as it was then called. Although many of my mostly white male colleagues were Ivy Leaguers, I gradually began to be recognized as a knowledgeable person, and even the "go-to person" to help colleagues deal with office, project management, and human relations issues. Finally, I was assigned as a junior Agricultural Attaché at the U.S. Mission to the European Union (USEC) in Brussels, Belgium, which was a real "feather in my cap" because this was one of the senior posts in US-European agricultural trade relations. Over time, with promotions to positions of higher responsibilities, both in Washington and on foreign assignments, I served as the Agricultural Counselor in the American Embassies in Bern, Switzerland and Rome, Italy.

GEM 24

Quite incredibly, after years of toiling in various positions at the USDA, I was appointed to the exalted position of Director General of the FAS' Foreign Service and then, as Agricultural Minister Counselor at the American Embassy in Paris, France. Wow! From being a lowly secretary to managing over 1,000 employees worldwide, with over a budget of over $100 million, was quite a journey from my childhood in Edgecombe, NC. It underscores that anything is possible when you are committed, work hard, and keep investing in learning and the improvement of self.

When at the zenith of my career, I was appointed to the position of U.S. Ambassador to the Central African Republic (CAR), the time had come for me to put everything I had done, all that I knew, and my desire to be "in service" into action. The appointment to this country, which is one of the poorest and most politically unstable in the world, was one of the greatest challenges in the service.

If anyone thought I couldn't handle it, though, they didn't know me, and they didn't understand what it took for me to ascend to this position. Failure was not an option.

So, I got into my role, deeply. Not content to sit back in the office on my laurels, I rolled up my sleeves and went out there and traveled the country as widely as possible to get to know the grassroots level of the society, and meet and engage with local elected officials. Few places were off-limits to me, and no task too small; I felt a true kinship with the people, and finally had the chance to do what I had wanted so many years ago, which was to work in an African country and serve people. I think the locals sensed my genuine connection with and affection for them because they named a school named in my honor. I was extremely sad when I had to depart my position prematurely due to an attempted coup-d'état.

When back on domestic soil, I rededicated myself to serving my family, church, staff, colleagues, neighbors, and the elderly. Today, having retired from a 41-year career in the government, I spend my time mentoring young professionals, giving inspirational speeches to high-school students, and serving in leadership positions in my AKA Chapter; in the National Coalition of "100 Black Women" that advocates for women and girls to thrive; and in the Association of Black American Ambassadors, working to ensure diversity in the U.S. Foreign Service.

When all is said and done, I know for sure that when you serve other people, you serve yourself. If I weren't "in service" what would I be, and how would I define my life and measure its importance?

I am not "in service" to receive accolades, although I have received many; I am in service to live in a way that adds value to others and meaning to my life.

GEM 24

Years from now, when people are traveling on US Highway 17 in Hampstead/Surf City/Edgecombe Township, Pender County, NC, which has been newly named "Ambassador Mattie R. Sharpless Highway," I hope they will learn from my example and remember: *"For to Whom Much is Given, Much is Expected."*

Gem 24 Essayist: **Ambassador Mattie R. Sharpless**

Ambassador Mattie R. Sharpless, an Independent Consultant, works to expand U.S./African agribusiness trade and investment. After a distinguished 4l-year career in the U.S. Department of Agriculture's (USDA) Foreign Agricultural Service (FAS), and a charter member of the U.S. Trade Representative's Trade Advisory Committee on Africa, she closely monitors and fosters U.S/African agricultural policies and trade relations. During her tenure as U.S. Ambassador to the Central African Republic, she gave priority emphasis to sustenance agricultural development. She served as FAS' Acting Administrator during the transition of Presidents Clinton and Bush Administrations, managing over 1,000 employees worldwide, and over a $100 million budget. She served as the Agricultural Minister Counselor, Agricultural Counselor, and Agricultural Attaché at the American Embassy in Paris, France, Rome, Italy, and at the U.S. Mission to the European Union in Brussels, Belgium, as well as Administrative Assistant at the U.S. Mission to the Organization of Economic Cooperation and Development, Paris, France, and in numerous senior positions at USDA Headquarters in Washington, D.C.. A native of Hampstead, NC, Ambassador Sharpless actively participates in the Alpha Kappa Alpha Sorority, Inc., the National Coalition of 100 Black Women, the Association of Black American Ambassadors, the DACOR House Foundation, and the North Carolina Central University Alumni Association. She holds a B.Sc. in Business Education from North Carolina College, and a MS in Business Administration and Economics from North Carolina Central University (NCCU). Among her numerous awards, are the Presidential Distinguished Service Award, the Presidential Meritorious Service Award, LBJ Living Legend Award, NCCU's Distinguished Alumni Award, NCCU's Shepard Medallion, the National Association for Equal Opportunity in Higher Education Distinguished Alumni Award, and the Designation of a portion of U.S Highway 17 in Hampstead/Surf City/Edgecombe, NC in her honor.

GEM 25

This I know for sure:
Career success is largely due to a sustained level of readiness for the next challenge and seizing opportunities with unwavering confidence.

I was born in 1952 in a village in the Parish of St. Michael, Barbados. My early memories are of a happy childhood being brought up in the comfort of a modern well-appointed home. My father, who had left school at the age of 14 and married my mother on his 21st birthday, made an indelible mark on me and the kind of person I have become. Both parents stressed the importance of obtaining a good education and made sure we did our school work and performed to the best of our abilities. The fact that I was only an average student was not their fault; they did everything in their power to help my brother and I succeed. Though my father was always busy with his various jobs and enterprises, he was an active and engaged father who both supported and disciplined us as required.

In striving for a better life, my parents emigrated to New York City in 1966. My brother and I stayed back until completion of secondary school and were looked after by our maternal grandmother. While the home of my grandmother was not well-appointed with all of the material comforts we had enjoyed in that of my parent's, it was filled with love and she filled us with an understanding and appreciation of our roots and of the broader aspects of our culture.

Once we joined our parents in America in 1970, my father made it very clear that he expected me to start working as soon as possible and to attend college while so doing. Getting a job was easier said than done. I applied for many jobs and was frustrated after being turned down so many times for jobs in Manhattan. I didn't know what to do but decided to try my luck on Flatbush Avenue in Brooklyn. I walked into the headquarters building of the Flatbush Savings Bank wearing my school blazer, a white shirt and tie, and gray slacks and politely asked to see someone in the Human Resources department so that I could apply for a job. I was granted an interview and though I don't remember much about it, I recall making it clear that I really needed a job and that I had recently arrived from Barbados. Empathy was shown to me and I was hired as a Trainee Teller and started the next day. In today's climate, one wonders if the same empathy would be shown to a young immigrant like myself?

I spent the next two years working fulltime at the Flatbush Savings Bank while attending Brooklyn College as an evening student. I struggled to pay the cost of tuition, however.

GEM 25

Miraculously, one day someone within my Caribbean Diaspora network who worked at the Commercial Bank, Manufacturers Hanover Trust (MHT), informed me of a great opportunity that would change my life. He told me that MHT offered tuition refunds for its employees who successfully completed courses that were relevant to banking. It took me a while but two years later, I was hired by MHT as a Teller at a slightly higher salary.

It worked out well all the way around. Since the branch to which I was assigned at MHT was far away from the college I was attending, I had to be extremely diligent to ensure that my "bank drawer" was balanced because I couldn't depart until it was. As I needed to take a couple of trains to get to school on time, I couldn't afford to have an "unbalanced drawer" because I would have had to stay late at work and then would have been late for my class. There is a reason I am mentioning this: It is to underscore the importance of doing one's job well and right the first time, because if you don't you may be too late to catch the train of life!

As the years went by and following the trauma of an armed robbery at my branch, I decided it was time to pursue a different role in banking; one that would enable me to apply my newly acquired knowledge and degree in Economics.

Fortunately, I had a mentor. He was my Branch Manager and he supported my ambition. Having already achieved Head Teller status, I was offered and accepted a position in an operations support role in the bank's International Division, which was located on Park Avenue in New York City. This move turned out to be a blessing in disguise because it exposed me to senior bankers in the division. This is where seizing opportunities makes all the difference: I immediately recognized the potential in the situation and stepped up my game in every way so that I could make the right impression and take advantage of the opportunity.

Here was another blessing and opportunity: I was conspicuous as one of very few black faces in the division. This enabled me to come to the attention of Dwight Allen, the Division Head, who took a personal interest in me and who was instrumental in my enrollment in the Management Training program of the Credit Analysis Department. This department was where the action was and being in it changed the trajectory of my career and led to even more exposure in the division. I made sure that what the "higher-ups" were seeing in my performance was excellence at every turn. As a result, I was selected for a short-term attachment to the Cairo Branch of MHT in 1979 to review their loan portfolio and to train staff in the fundamentals of credit analysis. Again, I recognized that I was in the spotlight and made sure that what they were seeing cast me in the most positive light.

GEM 25

Shortly after returning to New York, I was offered a three-year position in Singapore as Regional Head of Credit and I jumped at the chance, even though taking it required me to leave my family and friends. I had to make it work. I asked my fiancée to marry me, she agreed, and off we went to Singapore.

It wasn't easy, but what is? What it was, in fact, was a new world of opportunity, of new people, and new cultures, and I embraced it. Next, I moved into a business development position of the bank in Hong Kong, where I had even greater responsibility. Promotions to the positions of Vice President, Deputy Country Manager, and Managing Director came next during my eleven-year assignment in Hong Kong.

Yes, I was lucky, but luck alone without being prepared to take advantage of it doesn't produce success. What gets you over the finish line is doing the hard work and being prepared when opportunity knocks.

After Manufacturers Hanover merged with Chemical Bank, I was transferred to the Banking and Corporate Finance Division of Chemical Bank in New York in June 1994. Coincidently, whereas it had always been my dream to work in the bank's New York Headquarters, after so many years overseas, it was now a source of concern. After 14 years in Asia, I was out of touch with the domestic market in America. My path to continuing upward mobility was not clear. While I was finding my way, I focused on leveraging my Asia network as my key advantage. Along the way, I was approached by an Executive Search firm working on behalf of Standard Chartered Bank. The bank was looking for someone with precisely my experience in Asia to lead a team dedicated to the financial services needs of importers of textiles and apparel from the Asia Pacific Region. It was a perfect match and we succeeded in handling the trade business of major Hong Kong and China exporters and U.S. importers.

In the final chapter of my international banking career, I was given the opportunity to serve as the Country Chief Executive for Standard Chartered first in Nigeria, then Uganda, and Botswana. The latter was a tremendous feather in my cap because it was the bank's most profitable business in Sub-Saharan Africa in 2007 when I arrived.

After a 41-year career in banking, indeed I had come a long way from being a young lad walking into a bank in Brooklyn, without any references, and job experience—and being an immigrant—to positions in executive management of major banking operations in the U.S., Asia, and Africa. I was able to succeed because I was always prepared and ready to take advantage of any luck that came my way.

GEM 25

Today, as the current Honorary Consul for Barbados in Atlanta, Georgia, I am drawing on my experience to market the country of my birth as a destination for recreation and investment and am also assisting our Diaspora in Georgia and in the wider southeast region to propel them forward, as I was similarly propelled forward.

❖ ❖ ❖

Gem 25 Essayist: David Cutting

David D. Cutting is an international commercial banking professional with over 30 years of experience in North America, Asia, and Africa of which 12 years have been in Country Management. Until December 2010, he served as the Managing Director and Chief Executive Officer of the Standard Chartered Bank in Botswana, where he was responsible for the day to day management of the bank's business in Botswana. He also served as the Managing Director and Chief Executive Officer of Standard Chartered Bank Uganda Ltd (2004 -2007) and Standard Chartered Bank Nigeria Ltd (2000 – 2003).

Between 1994 and 2000 in New York, Mr. Cutting held the positions of Senior Vice President and Global Account Manager Corporate and Institutional Banking-Americas for Standard Chartered Bank, and Managing Director – Banking & Corporate Finance for Chemical Bank. In Asia between 1980 and 1994, he served as a Managing Director and Deputy Country Manager of what was Chemical Bank (now J P Morgan Chase) in Hong Kong, and as the Assistant Vice President and Credit Manager for Manufacturers Hanover's Singapore Branch, among various other positions throughout his distinguished international banking career.

Mr. Cutting earned a Bachelor of Arts degree in Economics from Brooklyn College City University of New York in 1976 and holds Diplomas in Bank Lending from the New York Institute of Credit and in Strategic Marketing Management from the Harvard University Graduate School of Business Administration. Today, Mr. Cutting is a private consultant and advisor to various organizations focused on sustainable development in Sub-Saharan Africa and the Caribbean where he was born and spent his formative years. He established Cutting Consulting Services, LLC in 2013 to market his knowledge of the Emerging Markets. In 2015, he was appointed Honorary Consul at Atlanta, Georgia for the Government of Barbados.

GEM 25

GEM 26

This I know for sure:
No matter what international development project you may be working on, the measure of its success is always about the people and your reward as a development agent is measured in terms of the positive interactions you have in working with the people to accomplish the objective.

I tell people I am from Italy, as the first 12 years or so of my life were spent there in a somewhat carefree peaceful existence on a small family farm my parents bought from my dad's mother. My dad had grown up on that same farm as one of seven children. Had I stayed there for high school, I would have been in a graduating class of around thirteen or so, but we moved. Good times in Italy: walking the pastures, hunting small game, fishing in the creek, riding to school with a one-armed bus driver. Different times…

My father returned from WWII and entered college to get his degree in Agricultural Economics. I would later follow in engineering – a choice fostered by my close relationship to my grandfather on my mother's side. During graduate school, I happened to sit by a person in an economics class and asked, "Are there any jobs you know about for an engineering aide?" Bingo! Within a week I was hired by the local electric utility where my classmate worked. Over the next 25 years, I worked for three separate utilities until I decided to move into consulting.

One day, I got a call from a former utility boss who asked: "Hey, are you still doing that consulting thing?" Long story short, by the following week, my wife and I had agreed to my taking a 10-month utility consulting job in Egypt for the U.S. Agency for International Development (USAID). This 10 month assignment turned into ten years. By then, I was firmly ensconced in the international developing arena and gladly accepted my next assignment in Armenia; it was followed by assignments in Jordan and Ukraine, before I returned to the U.S. to Washington, D.C. to support international development consulting efforts focused on a number of countries.

My experience overseas taught me that working environments are often defined by government, laws, cultures (both of citizenry and company origins), history, language, and prevailing relationships. Getting to the essence of these factors is part of the ramp-up process required to successfully "do business" in any country.

GEM 26

Perhaps the most challenging "ramp up" entails understanding the people. Working with a mix of people in a project environment (often of bi, if not, multi-cultural origins) presents a number of challenges. Paramount among these is trying to figure out what their sources of motivation are, understanding how to motivate them to work as a team, and learning what "flash points" to avoid. One of the most important things to figure out, however, is who has which contacts or leverage outside of the project and how to access their insights about how the project can be effective, and how I, as a manager, can be effective in managing the project?

There are a lot of "people" lessons to learn along the way. For instance, some countries have cultures that are very class conscious; some strive to emulate "western" values; while others have both hidden and obvious flash points. One thing is for sure: all have decades-old national and business practices that do not easily accept the "cultural changes" demanded by project goals, such as working outside of one's tribal/family norms; accepting the empowerment of women or perceived minority participants in solutions; getting over "zero sum" mentality to engage others in mutual benefit; being willing to "try something new" to achieve a desired outcome; etc. Leading or provoking change via project activities is further challenged by language differences – specifically a concern of this small-town, English-only-speaking person that I am.

It has been my experience that local foreign country staff support are generally excellent, or maybe I should say "could be generally excellent" – as many, though high-functioning in their current culture, did not have an initial broad grasp of what cultural changes they can be a part of, nor of their own "cultural changes" they will likely make along the way. Over the years, seeing what I perceived as a vast level of untapped resource capability that lay in the local staff, I began to proactively pursue a variety of "personal growth" efforts targeting certain individuals in addition to our targeted project beneficiaries.

One day while walking through our project's large staging area, where literally thousands of computers were being loaded with educational software for schools, I stopped to pick up some packing materials that were hindering workers moving units around. Later, one of the senior staff noted their "ah-ha!" moment of becoming part of the change when seeing me do that – "…if the head of the project takes time to pick up things, maybe I should also, though I am the leader of this computer preparation group."

Along the same lines, I once had an administrative manager who came from a socially well-placed family. She knew people who knew people, and had a great work ethic, though little experience. The growth path for this manager was learning how to

GEM 26

leverage others, not just because of tribal/family connections, but by engaging them in supporting project goals. This person is now Chief of Staff for one of the largest financial institutions in the country.

Earlier, I mentioned language being important. Here, I am not just referring to the simple translation of words, but rather the use of language to convey meaning, intent, nuance – all within cultural sensitivities. Some of the most impressive personal growth successes I have witnessed are those of translators and interpreters. I spent a great deal of time with them in providing the broader background for the bases of my comments. Gradually, they became more familiar with the logic behind the collections of statements they were translating – hopefully making more certain that those listening/reading in their own language got a more productive idea of the concepts discussed.

Their individual exposures and receptivity to personal growth has positively correlated with their current successes in many cases, I have noted. For instance, one person is now a project manager with a U.S. consulting firm; another is continuing to provide translation services directly to the U.S. Government and one has a senior position bridging government and business; yet another has moved into government representation at the international level.

International development work typically takes place in or between two nodes – helping the most needy or helping businesses or government entities become more successful. I have project experiences across this spectrum and can attest to the different approaches involved. What is common, however, is the bond that forms between the people irrespective of position and cultures. We meld into a family of sorts, with common goals. I have sat on a porch chewing sugar cane while dozens of kids ran around; I have eaten at a newspaper-covered table while drinking the only Coke in the residence; I've held the hands of grieving parents, walked farm fields and pastures, toured beloved historical sites, responded to requests to polish resumes as persons seek to move their careers forward, prepared a gift photo of a deceased child, assisted family businesses to make previously unconceivable changes, trained in casual and formal settings; and been blessed many times by a quiet "thank you" or hug. Who were these men and women? They are drivers, entrepreneurs, facilities cleaners, senior government and business officials, project staff and spouses, regulators, farmers, local religious officials, career professionals, neighborhood leaders, school teachers and administrators, shopkeepers, mechanics, mute parking assistants, the wealthy, the poor, the educated, and the illiterate.

GEM 26

Institutions come and go: some are affected by government actions, some evolve over time by owner or employee factors, some are productive, some stagnate, some become redundant, and some vanish. Obviously, there is a range of impacts these institutions (family farms, businesses, schools, government, factories, service entities, etc.) can have on or be affected by the people they touch over time. However, more so than institutions, people interacting with people is the route to provoke positive change and secure environments that are broadly beneficial. To be a provoker of positive change frequently requires one to also change – accepting others' starting points, respecting cultural norms, transcending one's own personal boundaries, etc. "Achieving success is always about the people" you get to work with. Oh, in the above specific examples, all were women except one, and did I say that was Italy, Texas?

✦ ✦ ✦

Gem 26 Essayist: **Larry Hearn**

Mr. Hearn is an engineer and project manager with more than 40 years of domestic and international experience, serving industry and government. He has held senior positions in both government-owned and investor-owned utility organizations. He has broad professional experience as a senior decision-maker working in small and large organizational structures and in the US, Eastern Europe, and the Middle East. In addition to engineering, his expertise includes management, education, and human and institutional capacity development. As an international project manager and development specialist, consultant and trainer, Mr. Hearn's experience has ranged from working on large multi-component USAID projects that necessitated balancing conflicting agendas among partners and the host government, to working in small and large private sector organizations. Mr. Hearn is widely regarded for his leadership and team building skills and for developing and managing a diverse client base of projects. His expertise includes management, private sector business relationship development, public-private partnerships, human development, and team-building among clients and partners in a variety of environments.

Mr. Hearn currently serves as a Board Member and Vice-President for a non-governmental organization that seeks to share knowledge and services to help water and sanitation utilities in development countries. He holds an undergraduate degree in Mechanical Engineering from Texas A&M University, a graduate degree in Education from the University of North Texas, and an MBA in Production Management from the University of Texas at Austin.

GEM 26

GEM 27

This I know for sure:
You have to come to a fundamental understanding of yourself before you can authentically support the development of others.

My life began just a few miles from our nation's capital as the Cold War faded into the shadows, the decade of President Ronald Reagan and Mayor Marion Barry began, and the "War on Drugs" and crack took center stage in the District of Columbia (D.C.).

We were a typical lower-middle-income family. Like most American families at the time, mine was "house-poor," and my father worked long hours fighting to achieve the American dream. Only one thing made us different to other families: My father was a single parent in the 1980s, even though he was not a widow. Although the courts usually grant custody to mothers in divorce proceedings, in our case, because our mother chose a life of drugs, while our father was prepared to be a full-time parent and provider, he was awarded custody of my siblings and me.

As drugs and violence increasingly claimed our inner cities, our father decided that it was time to move us to a neighborhood just outside Raleigh, North Carolina in the rural south to escape the challenges of life in the D.C. area.

The culture shock of arriving in North Carolina cannot be overstated. I remember coming home after the first day of school in the fifth grade and asking my father, "Where are all the black people?" Our school was 95% white, while in Maryland, it had been 95% black. Overnight, I went from being in the minority to being in the majority, and I wasn't prepared for the shift in power that ensued. Looking back, while in elementary school in Maryland, I cannot remember a single time when I thought of my own race, or what it meant to be white; I was treated like everyone else, and I treated people the way I was treated. Maybe I was too young to understand or recognize the subtle or even overt injustices around me.

When we got to North Carolina, my world changed. Our community there was comprised of predominantly upper-middle-class white people; people of color were treated differently in public, and it was clear that white people were in a position of power. My black teacher was called names by some students when they were angry about a grade or being disciplined. Not only had I never seen teachers being disrespected before, I also had not experienced a teacher who seemed so angry all the time. My black teacher was curt, strict, and unable to emotionally connect to students. I thought she hated me. At the time, I was too naive to understand that she had spent a lifetime being oppressed and hurt because of the color of her skin.

Throughout school, I gradually learned how racial oppression had transformed the entire world, while in my corner of it, I saw how it plays out in everyday life and affects community development.

When I entered college, although I didn't know what I would do with my life, I knew that I wanted to create a more just and peaceful world for everyone. As my studies progressed, I learned more about the many forms of oppression, including those which pertain to race, class, gender, geography, ethnicity, and sexual orientation. Not only did I learn about their pervasiveness, I also examined how systems of oppression are formed and perpetuated, and how the intersection of identities creates additional layers of oppression. Eventually, my studies took me outside the United States to places where layers of oppression from colonialism still linger. My commitment to fighting for change intensified.

As I began my career in international development, I felt it was my duty as a global citizen to help those in need and by the time I was 33, I had lived or worked in more than two dozen countries around the world on health and education projects aimed at lifting people out of poverty and helping them to use their voice to self-advocate for change. I was passionate about my work and prior to commencing any assignment, I engaged in extensive research on the cultures of the countries in which I'd be working because I wanted to identify and understand the nuances and mechanisms of oppression in each society. I'm proud to say that the programs I developed were evidence-based and culturally sensitive.

After some time in the field overseas, I returned to the U.S. to attend graduate school at American University (AU) in D.C, where I studied International Education. My studies helped me to critically analyze the U.S.'s role in international development and understand that while U.S. foreign assistance funds are often used for altruistic purposes, they are also abused for political ends as well. Inevitably, the U.S. always stands to gain the most from this duality.

In the course of several years reflecting on my work in international development, I have gone over the meetings I have had, analyzed the programs I have helped to design with local partners, and pondered about the interactions I have had with people while traveling; I have come to the conclusion that in many ways, I have unknowingly perpetuated the "white savior complex." This was not my intention; my aim was to build interpersonal relationships based on trust.

GEM 27

Taking a step back even further to reflect on my experience as a teenager, I have gleaned some deeper insights into myself. I grew up at the time of the "Don't Ask, Don't Tell" era in the mid-1990s and when I travelled overseas, I carried this ideology with me. If people didn't ask me, I wouldn't tell them I was gay, nor that I was married to an amazing woman. I played the pronoun game like a champ and dodged questions about not having children, allowing people to conclude that it was because I was focusing on my career. While some people thought it was odd that I was single and didn't have a boyfriend, many others genuinely respected and trusted me, and didn't seek to delve further. As a "queer" woman, I inadvertently perpetuated the false dichotomy that it is okay to "queer" and closeted; by not presenting my true authentic self, the trust I built with people was not built on the unadulterated truth of who I am.

I also came to realize that I have missed opportunities to more effectively leverage my power as a white American working on international development projects because I didn't yet have the tools, skills, or courage needed to support people on their own terms, and not just promote the American agenda. I lacked these internal resources because I had not yet developed "authentic" trusting relationships with those with whom I was working; without such relationships, I was only able to perpetuate the power dynamics of colonialism and oppression that they had experienced their entire lives. Some people may have known I was gay, but they didn't learn it directly from me, and that's unfortunate.

Today, I am armed with a deeper understanding of my power and privilege as a white American living in the U.S., while as an acknowledged "queer" woman, I finally feel like my authentic self and able to engage in the work that supports the kind of change I truly believe in for the betterment of others. Now, I'm ready to go outside my comfort zone and take bigger risks that could help to bring about significant change for those most impacted by racism, colonialism, patriarchy, white supremacy, xenophobia, homophobia, and hyper-capitalism. What I know for sure is that for real change to occur, we must confront and challenge ourselves first, and only then can we address the people, policies, and systems that maintain privileges that promote power for white people to the exclusion of others.

✦ ✦ ✦

GEM 27

Gem 27 Essayist: **Sarah N. Dunn Phillips**

Mrs. Dunn Phillips is an burgeoning entrepreneur focused on supporting socially just oriented individuals and institutions to build a more just and peaceful world. She has worked in over 25 countries during the past 19 years focusing on creating higher education and economic opportunities for marginalized populations. As an expert on ecosystems for creating positive for change and growth around the world, her services have been retained by leading development institutions, corporations, foreign countries, and others for almost two decades. She will soon publish her first book on hidden LGBT voices. She holds undergraduate degrees from Meredith College and graduate degree from American University.

GEM 27

GEM 28

This I know for sure: *Understanding and accepting diversity has made me a better person and more productive throughout my career, fostering greater collaboration among my many colleagues.*

I am an immigrant, born in Cuba of parents who were originally from Spain. In late 1957, we emigrated from Cuba to the U.S., just before the 1959 Cuban Revolution. My quest to understand diversity began with my recognition of my own ethnic difference in the small town in rural Illinois in which we lived, where there was limited diversity in our community. I stood out, but mostly fitted in.

Although I was an average student, I had boundless curiosity and a desire to understand the world around me, especially that which pertained to issues of diversity. I recall reading books in the seventh grade such as *Black Like Me* and *Manchild in the Promised Land*. The latter was especially impactful on me as a 12-year-old; it was set in Harlem during the 1950s, and explained some of the challenges facing black Americans in urban settings like Harlem, which were marked at the time by violence, police brutality, and other ills. Collectively, these books deepened and broadened my understanding of American life and demonstrated that the notion of equality was still an aspirational goal.

My first heroes were Martin Luther King and Robert F. Kennedy. Later in life, I came to know about Cesar Chavez and began following his movement that aimed to improve the lives of Mexican farm workers; my own small contribution was that I began to boycott grapes. Looking back, I can map my journey on my road to a better understanding of other races and cultures, and how mine fitted into the overall scheme.

When I enrolled in a small liberal arts college in Davenport, Iowa, I finally had an opportunity to broaden my knowledge and awareness, and one of the first things I did was to change my name back to Juan from the Americanized version, "John." My closest friend back then was Tony Clark, who later became Father Tony Clark, a Catholic priest.

Tony helped me in my journey of discovery, and introduced me first-hand to a new world that I had only known through television and books. We volunteered at "Friendly House," an inner-city youth center for African-Americans, while on weekends, we visited migrant camps that housed hundreds of Mexicans. These experiences transformed me, and served to open my eyes to the injustices in society. They also

GEM 28

led me to take on a proactive role, speaking out and fighting against discrimination and inequality.

After completing my undergraduate degree, I immediately enrolled in graduate school at American University in Washington, D.C. where I majored in International Affairs, focusing on Latin American studies. My roommate was from Cameroon. Mulu Tamungang would often play records with African rhythms that featured drums and congas; this reminded me of Cuban music, which has origins in Africa. In addition to learning about African music, Mulu taught me about West Africa and African culture.

American University was a melting pot of cultures and home to students from about 130 cultures. The university's student center was a "mini United Nations" where the sound of languages from Farsi to Arabic and Spanish to French was heard on a regular basis. While matriculating, I continued on my personal journey by helping marginalized communities and volunteering on Tuesdays at "Ayuda," a non-profit that supported immigrants' rights. Every time I went there, I felt like Dorothy in The Wizard of Oz, observing "We are not in Kansas anymore."

After completing my graduate degree, I was hired by the U.S. Government Accountability Office (GAO), and by the age of 26, was able to realize my dream of working overseas. I was recruited to serve in GAO's Latin America office in Panama, where my work covered a total of 23 countries under its purview, involving highly politically sensitive projects. My life in Latin America during those years was culturally rich and rewarding, and it was enriching to experience diverse cultures, languages, and foods, and to have the opportunity to learn about the history and traditions of each country; this all added to my own "treasure trove" of knowledge and global understanding. On a professional level, I also learned a lot, and had the opportunity to work on consequential international economic projects that involved foreign governments and NGO stakeholders.

During my eight years with the GAO, I had the privilege of serving under four female managers, from whom I also learned a lot. Hiring females for higher-level positions was an example of affirmative action that was good and positive, and made a difference. This was in the 1980s, when American society made great strides in recognizing and appreciating many forms of diversity. After the GAO, I was hired by PriceWaterhouseCoopers (PWC) as a manager for its consulting practice based in Honduras. At PWC, I was considered "diverse," and my diversity was an asset for the company because I am bilingual. My prior experience working with the U.S. Government programs in Latin America was also an asset.

GEM 28

Having been overseas and then returned to the U.S., I focused on promoting business and global trade, while as the President of the Greater Washington Hispanic Chamber of Commerce, one of my key goals was to identify procurement opportunities for Hispanic firms with corporate America and the U.S. Government. My experience with diversity programs was helpful here because major corporations often set aside certain goods and services to be purchased from minority firms. The work wasn't easy but it was rewarding, especially when connections and business were successfully facilitated.

Currently, I live in southern New Mexico, where I run a consulting practice that develops and promotes Latino micro-enterprises. When I reached the age of 60, I became a substitute teacher, and find great joy in working with students with learning disabilities. My wife Claudia, my soulmate and teacher, has taught me about the challenges of life along the border and the struggles of the Mexican people, and together, we do what we can to help.

Unfortunately, although I have dedicated my entire life to promoting diversity, I find that appreciation for such an approach is at a low point in American society. Despite this, I know for sure that when people take the time to open their hearts and minds to diversity, they are laying a foundation for peace, unity, and prosperity.

✦ ✦ ✦

GEM 28

Gem 28 Essayist: Juan Albert

With 37 years of professional experience, Juan Albert's assignments has taken him to 35 countries throughout Latin America, Europe and Asia. Juan Albert is currently partner and founder of New Mexico Borderworx, an international management consulting firm. His past professional careers involved stints with the U.S. Government Accountability Office (GAO), PricewaterhouseCoopers (PWC), President of the Greater Washington Hispanic Chamber of Commerce, along with starting two companies. Juan is a social entrepreneur and has served on a total of 15 boards including those pertaining to minority business development, international trade, women empowerment, education, and tourism. Juan has a B.A. in Political Science and Psychology from St. Ambrose University, Davenport, IA, and a M.A. in International Affairs from the American University, Washington, D.C. He is the father of four children, Juan, Marisa, Javier, and Adriana. He currently resides in Las Cruces, NM with his wife Claudia. For more information on New Mexico Borderworx visit: (*www.nmborderworx.com*).

GEM 29

This I know for sure:
It was my inability to successfully plan my life that landed me in destinations that were exactly where I should have been.

Circuitous routes and events guided my life's journeys and, in the end, landed me precisely where I should have been.

At an early age, due to unplanned circumstances, I suddenly found myself living in California. I was a native-born Texan and spent most of my adult life trying to return there from places I found myself in. As a young Black American, I could have never imagined that I would wind up living in and loving Far East Asia for the better part of my adult life.

Here is how it happened. As a child, I was taken from my home to California to live with my grandparents. Initially, I was told that it was "just for a little while" but that turned into essentially forever. I devised what I thought was a perfect plan to return to my beloved Texas and family. It involved joining the U. S. Navy, so I could be free to determine my own destination. To my disappointment, my naval career took me even further west away from the Rio Grande River and Texas.

My tours of duty in the navy took me to Hawaii, San Diego, California, Guam USA, then back to San Diego, followed by Vietnam, and back to San Diego yet again.

In these places, as a young Black American, I experienced being the "first" in various regards. In Hawaii, for instance, I was the youngest sailor (Black or White) to be granted a Top Secret (Special Intelligence) security clearance. In San Diego, I was given responsibility for the communications facilities for the Naval Investigative Service Offices (NISO). In Guam, I was be assigned to TWO separate air squadrons simultaneously, which may even have been a first for the U. S. Navy. The two air squadrons included a weather squadron, Airborne Early Warning Squadron ONE, and the other was a Top-Secret intelligence gathering squadron. In Vietnam, I was assigned as a senior petty officer to the Intelligence Division on the staff of the Commander, U.S. Naval Forces in Vietnam.

I was 32 years old by the time I finally returned to Houston for the first time since childhood. Even then, it was only for a brief visit while I was in route to Washington,

33 Gems ✦ Wisdom for Living Pieces of Life's Puzzle

D.C. to prepare for my subsequent Attaché assignments. My first such assignment was at the U. S. Embassy in Tel Aviv.

I still had a plan to return to live in Houston, Texas, but when I retired from military service. Following my assignment in Israel, the Navy had a different plan for me, however. I was informed that I was needed in the British Colony of Hong Kong and then in Beijing, China. It was now 1976 and yet again, though I longed to be in Texas, I was in the Far East and closer to California than to Texas. At the time, I had no idea that Hong Kong was about to become my home – FOR A VERY LONG TIME!

Up to this point, all of my attempts at planning my life had been a total failure. When I was released from the U.S. Navy, I was 39 years old. Although a job awaited me in the garment industry in San Diego, California, I remained in the Far East to serve the U.S. Government. While the period of my "normal" enlistment had ended, the U. S. Government involuntarily and unexpectedly extended my service "for the convenience of the government" and assigned me to an eight-month term in Beijing, The People's Republic of China. I was there when I had a chance to greet our Envoy, George H.W. Bush, and his "beautiful wife" Barbara upon their visit to China.

Looking back on my childhood in California, I recall my grandfather's words. He said, (using an old slave saying): "there is no such thing as can't. They" (Dim folks in power) done killed can't and ran the hell out of couldn't"). Most of my life, I tried to heed this wise anecdote and believed there "was nothing that a Black man couldn't do." This attitude and outlook enabled me to embrace my new civilian life in the Far East. I came to "own it" and everyone came to know Jim Harvey.

The Navy assigned me to Beijing in 1978. Using my knowledge of The People's Republic of China, I became the first businessperson in the world to pioneer household goods forwarding in China. My knowledge of the Far East and the fact that I was a Black American were assets in my relationship with the Chinese authorities. I was told that they were "honored" that I was Black and could therefore be trusted as a faithful business partner. I was required to offer my services to the Third World countries as well. This was a "no brainer" requirement for me. At last, I was finally where I should have been.

I became an international industry expert for shipments to The People's Republic of China; The Republic of Mongolia; and The Democratic People's Republic of Korea (DPRK), and over, the years have become unforgettable in the international household transportation industry. Everyone knows "China Jim (gem)!

GEM 29

As a 77-year-old Black American, Texan in Hong Kong, I am now definitely where I should be. I have learned that one shouldn't plan too much and that there is no such thing as can't"! "Anywhere you are is home. "Slow down and enjoy the trip, and remember, "A smile is contagious"!

❖ ❖ ❖

Gem 29 Essayist: **Jim Harvey**

Jim Harvey retired from the U.S. Navy after 22 years of active service. He attended the Monterey Union High School in Monterey, California and obtained an associate degree at San Diego City College. He obtained a Bachelor of Arts in Applied Arts and Sciences and Public Administration from San Diego State University, San Diego, California. He spent over ten years working in the international logistics industry and has resided and worked in Hong Kong for 42 years. He pioneered the household goods industry in The People's Republic of China and the Republic of Mongolia.

GEM 29

GEM 30

This I know for sure:
Music is a healing force in the universe.

I grew up in Philadelphia in the 1950's when African Americans were beginning to branch out into parts of the city that were being newly integrated. I remember a few white folks that hadn't moved from my neighborhood yet and one of them had a pool table in his basement. When his house was sold, the pool table remained, and the new owners invited my father and some of the other men in the neighborhood to come over and socialize, play pool, and enjoy each other's company. A new day was dawning.

Nevertheless, some things remained the same. My mother's plight was part of the same story of many black women of her time: She had to stay home to take care of the kids, but she also needed to make money to maintain the household. She did all that she could, from taking care of children, to sewing, to working for a white man who used to bring boxes of stockings over for her to sort through to identify imperfections. Her industriousness was a good role model for me. Like her, I'd always be on the lookout for how to make a buck for the rest of my life.

My father worked for the government and was also a trained vocalist. He was paid as a soloist to sing at a church on Sundays and on special holidays. We always had music in our home and listened to musicians like Count Basie, Duke Ellington, Ella Fitzgerald, Sarah Vaughn, Nat King Cole, and to many other great black singers and musicians of the day.

Starting in the 1930s, Philadelphia became an important city for music and musicians, especially for hand drummers. Such drummers were heavily influenced by music from Africa and the Caribbean. On occasion, they performed in New York where they joined other African American, African, and Caribbean drummers. Personally, I was drawn to the music of drums from the first time I heard them; they drew me in and made me want to join in. When I heard the famous drummer Olatunji's "Drums of Passion", I was hooked and knew that playing the drums would be part of my future.

In my neighborhood, our heroes were the Jazz musicians who lived nearby and those who had moved from New York to Philadelphia to get away from the hustle and bustle of the city. All of these experiences opened my world to music and set the tone for my future.

GEM 30

I attended the Pennsylvania Academy of Fine Arts for a few years, but the love of the drum was in my heart. Once I put together the concept of using congas and percussion instruments in commercial music, I was ready to pursue my career. At first, I played with local bands in town and eventually began going to New York to "sit in" to play with different bands. In the beginning it was rough, most African American hand drummers couldn't get "gigs" with Latin bands because they only wanted Latin drummers. I didn't let that stop me, however. I found a way to pursue my passion for playing the conga drums by distinguishing my approach; I used a variety of percussion instruments to enhance the music beyond merely using the conga drums.

As I continued my path in music over the years, I experienced firsthand just how hard it was to make a living in this business. Frequent rejection is a fact of life and major obstacle to overcome. Being able to handle it and use rejection as a source of energy, is key. Fortunately, I had my mother's support from the very beginning to help me stay strong and not give up. My dad was not supportive in the beginning, however; he had wanted me to complete college and become anything other than a musician or artist. Eventually, he came around once he realized how important music was to me and how determined I was to succeed.

Despite the all the challenges associated with trying to make it in the music industry, I have managed to have an incredible career and have performed with famous artists from various genres, while touring around the world. Some of the places we performed were like experiencing a live version of National Geographic. The best part, of course, was meeting people from many different walks of life. The drum took me around the world.

In 1997, I was offered the position of Musical Director for a popular cooking show on the Food Network. This opportunity introduced me to another level of music…in television! Doing the show required a whole new approach to music to accommodate it to the requirements of television.

This was the first time the network had live music on any of its shows, and it was the first time an all African American band was viewed on a regular basis on any network. We went through some changes. But, overall, it was a great experience performing with guest artists, eating incredible food, and being viewed around the world. It was bittersweet though; the executive producer and I never connected. We always knocked heads, which made going to work a real job. To make matters worse, on the set the chef gave the impression that we were best friends, like brothers, but off set,

GEM 30

unfortunately, he went one way, and I went the other. This is exactly the opposite of how musicians interact and flow in a situation.

The show ended December 2007 after a ten-year run, and thus ended another chapter in my journey.

It was time to reinvent myself once again. Throughout my career I have always been involved in educating students in public and private schools, doing assembly programs, residencies, and workshops. I thought this would be the perfect transition after the show. Unfortunately, music and the arts had all but disappeared from public schools and there were very few schools that could afford any extra programs. A further disadvantage I faced was that my instrument was no longer being used in today's music and because the use of sampled electronic music predominates, there was very little work for me in my profession in Philadelphia.

Time for another reinvention. My new focus was on healing through music. It wasn't a far stretch because I truly believed that whenever there is adversity, music can be a healing force. Philadelphia wasn't the place to branch out in this direction, however, so in 2015, I relocated to Los Angeles. I wasn't sure what turn my career would take but I let the drum lead me and take me on my next adventure.

A year after arriving in Los Angeles, I created, "Healing Sound Therapy" using my instruments for meditation, relieving stress, promoting inner harmony, and reconnecting the mind, body, and spirit. So far, I have presented my sound therapy to Alzheimer's patients, to senior citizens who were living in senior care facilities, and have used it in yoga studios and in private sessions. Those who have experienced it have said that they felt a connection to the energy created by the instruments and that it made them feel relaxed and at peace. We all need love, peace, and harmony in our lives and one input for achieving these positive states in through letting healing music into our hearts, minds, souls. Music is truly a healing force in the universe.

✦ ✦ ✦

Gem 30 Essayist: "Baba Doc" (Leonard Gibbs)

Following his highly successful musical career of national, international touring, and recording as lead percussionist in the bands of high profile vocalists including Al Jarreau, Anita Baker, Dianne Reeves, and Erykah Badu, and being a key musician in the rhythm sections of bands including those of Grover Washington Jr. , Bob James, Ricki Lee Jones, Wyclef Jean and many others, master drummer and percussionist Baba Doc Gibbs heard a new rhythm. New directions called to Baba Doc, and he drew on his musical experiences to create a program of healing musical groups and individual musical sounds to promote healing. This was an easy and natural transition for him.

Looking back, it was Grover Washington Jr. whose understanding of the healing properties of music gave a young percussionist from Philadelphia, Leonard Gibbs, the honorific title "Doctor". Grover's vision saw that his percussionist was a "Doctor of Sounds".

From 1997-2007, Baba Doc Gibbs was the musical director for the popular cooking show, "Emeril Live" on the Food Network, where he brought his healing sounds to the master chef and thousands of viewers worldwide.

Sound has been used as a powerful healing mechanism since humans first formed civilizations that promoted high level spiritual consciousness. The first rhythm we feel and sounds we hear come to us while we are in the stress-free womb of our mothers. This experience unifies all humans no matter race, gender, age, or religious belief system.

Sound therapists have the ability to use sound frequencies to interact with the energy frequencies of human bodies. Through these interactions, frequencies, and energy, the human body can be balanced.

Recognizing the importance of healing with sound, "Baba Doc" created the "Healing Sound Bath" using a variety of percussion instruments that each have a unique voice and energy to create an experience that promotes relaxation, stress relief, healing, breathing, and balances both hemispheres of the brain.

GEM 30

Participants experience the soothing energy of gongs, cymbals, and meditation bells. "Baba Doc" provides additional colors and feelings to the experience as he plays his ocean drum, rain stick, *kamale ngoni*, and the hand pan among others instruments.

"Baba Doc's" *Healing Sound Bath* provides relief from daily stress and promotes deep relaxation. It releases negative energy and emotions, helps reconnect mind, body and spirits, and assists in recovery after illness. *Healing Sound Bath* can be created, performed, and presented in yoga studios, meditation centers, senior citizen facilities, artists' lofts; and for corporations, as well as for the benefit of Alzheimer patients and special needs communities.

GEM 30

GEM 31
This I know for sure:
Creativity can be a pathway to joy.

We are all creative beings. When we were children, making up games, imaginary friends, stories, songs, and visual art were part of our daily activities that gave us joy. As we grew up, we were told that we had to think and behave a certain way and that our art even had to look a certain way. We were told that engaging in our creative activities was not the best use of our time. Instead, we needed to focus on our multiplication tables and memorizing words for the spelling bee and not on our creative activities. Despite all of the messages to the contrary, I found then, and still now, that creative outlets provide energy and are a respite from the daily grind.

I have also found that taking time to do something creative makes me more productive and efficient in my job. Consequently, I have advised friends and relatives to find a creative outlet unrelated to their professions. It is a good and necessary thing and allows the mind to wander, relax, and come up with imaginative solutions to seemingly intractable problems.

For me, art is like breathing. I can't live without it! There has never been a time in my life when I have not been drawing or painting ideas that popped into my head. When my images also provide joy and comfort to others that is a bonus.

My earliest "art" memories are of my mother, Linnet E. Farrell, keeping me quiet in church by drawing something on a pad she kept in her purse. After she drew something, she would give the pad to me, indicating that it was my turn. During these times, I was transported to another realm and to a wonderfully peaceful place. When my late father, Arthur T. Farrell, would ask me what I wanted for Christmas or for my birthday, the answer was always the same—a "paint-by-numbers set." I painted so often and intensely that there wasn't enough paint in the set and I was frustrated when it ran out before I could fill in all the numbers. Over time, friends and relatives helped made sure that I received lots of art supplies and I was able to draw to my heart's content.

When it became clear that I was interested in a career in the arts, teachers helped me create a portfolio for my application to New York's High School of Art & Design. The school, located in mid-town Manhattan's advertising district, trained students for commercial and theatre art careers. It was in my advertising and illustration classes

GEM 31

in school where I learned about gouache painting (similar to watercolors), which has been my preferred medium ever since.

After completing high school, I studied art and art history at State University of New York in New Paltz. Following my father's practical advice, I also earned a master's degree in library science at the Pratt Institute. My father had counseled me that while it was fine to be an artist, I should get a job with a pension and benefits, just in case.

My father and mother emigrated to the United States from Panama after World War II. My paternal uncle was the first to move to the U.S. and was the one who petitioned for the rest of his family to emigrate. Not about to let the love of her life get away, my mother got her aunt in New York to sponsor her so that she could join my dad. They married in New York soon thereafter.

When family members talked about life "back home" in Panama it made me curious about the wider world. Although they clearly missed many things about life in Panama, they also indicated that we were fortunate to live in the "land of opportunity." My two sisters and I heard that message loud and clear, which is probably why we pursued public service careers.

While working in the Brooklyn Public Library was enjoyable, the idea of living and working abroad was always on my mind. On the advice of a supervisor, I contacted the U.S. Information Agency and eventually applied to and joined the Foreign Service. The result was a rewarding career in cultural diplomacy and media relations.

My knowledge of art was an asset in my career in the Foreign Service. As an artist, many doors opened to me that may not have otherwise. In other countries, artists are respected and are often influential members of their societies. In meeting and getting to know artists, I gleaned additional insights into the society and about its values. In turn, when people saw my artwork, they felt that I had taken the time to get to know their country and what made it unique. It showed that I cared. The vibrancy of the societies and cultures in Africa and Latin America provided endless artistic inspiration.

Over the years, I found that bright colors could also be healing. In the summer of 2001, I was busily working on a number of pieces for a solo show at the former Parish Gallery, located in Georgetown, Washington, D.C.. The opening reception was scheduled for September 21, 2001. Then 9/11 happened. I asked the late Norm Parish if we should still go ahead with the opening. He felt that it was needed and he was right! Some of my friends from New York attended and said that they were glad. The artwork was a vibrant and cheerful tonic for that difficult time. From that day on, creating work to lift other's spirits became my mission.

GEM 31

Our world is full of rich, beautiful colors. My goal as an artist is to record beauty. In the process, I hope my art will bring joy into the viewer's life.

Most of us are looking for ways to make life better for future generations. And while we all may be facing challenges, we live with the faith that tomorrow will be better, as we seek ways to build bridges of understanding. We must also deal with those who are bent on destruction and discord, bombarded as we are with reports of unspeakable horror caused by forces of nature or by human frailties. Yet, even in the midst of this chaos, one can find beauty, peace and comfort.

My mission is to record as much of life's beauty as possible, using the richest color combinations that I can devise. My goal is to remember that every day there are more individuals acting out of love and kindness than hate. I tell their stories to inspire and comfort others.

✦ ✦ ✦

Gem 31 Essayist: **Cynthia Farrell Johnson**

Cynthia Farrell Johnson is a fan of vibrant colors. Her works in gouache, acrylic, and mixed media have been inspired by the people she met and places where she lived during 25 years of globetrotting as a U.S. diplomat. Service in West Africa, Central and South America exposed her to a wide variety of artistic traditions and forms of expression. Her role models are Romare Bearden, Jacob Lawrence, Faith Ringgold and Vincent Van Gogh. Johnson currently makes her home in Silver Spring, Maryland, and draws much of her inspiration for themes and color schemes from the Washington, D.C. region's rich, cultural diversity.

In July 2013, Johnson was awarded an Arts and Humanities Council of Montgomery County Individual Artist/Scholar Grant. Johnson was Artist-in-Residence at Wesley Theological Seminary's Luce Center for the Arts & Religion in 2011. Two years prior to that, she was Artist-in-Residence at Iona Senior Services.

Johnson's paintings have been exhibited overseas in cultural centers and galleries in Africa and in Latin America. As a participant in the U.S. Department of State's Art in Embassies Program, Ms. Johnson has placed her work in the U.S. ambassadorial residence in Niger, Nicaragua, Serbia, Ecuador, El Salvador, and Panama.

To learn more, visit: (*www.cfjfinearts.com*).

GEM 31

GEM 32

This I know for sure:
Creative endeavors are much more than hobbies; they feed our souls, relationships, and pocketbooks.

I grew up in a home with parents who ran a professional consulting practice out of the basement of our home, many years before "work from home" became fashionable (circa 1973). Creative problem-solving was part of our everyday routine, which is an experience that has served me well in my business career. Both of my parents believed in continuing their education and obtained graduate degrees in adulthood: my mother went back to school at 50 years of age to obtain a Master's degree in a field that involved creative problem-solving, and my father obtained a Ph.D. in Organizational Communications. The entire family was involved in creative problem-solving meetings for the family business on Sunday evenings.

To feed our right brains, the creative side, my brother and I were encouraged to try our skills at creative after-school activities; in my case, this entailed piano, ballet, baton and classical drama lessons. I loved to write and found that poetry was a wonderful outlet for my emotional growth. I applied my creativity in the papers I wrote while at university. For instance, my undergraduate college thesis was entitled "Anti-Semitism in 20th Century American Black literature". I am a Lebanese-Italian American.

After obtaining an undergraduate degree in English and History and an MBA in International Business and Marketing, my professional career in the corporate sector began in earnest. In the early years of my career, my entrepreneurial and creative problem-solving approach put me in a good position to find a place on the ground floor of the "new business" side of a major telecommunications company. My position entailed helping the company invest in entrepreneurial ventures, and in this regard I helped to lead the company's international expansion. As a result, I was the firm's first home-grown managing director located in Asia; I achieved this position when I was just 26 years of age.

When I returned to the U.S. from Asia, I landed in a very traditional but supposedly *"creative"* job working with major advertising agencies to oversee marketing communications. Creative it was not! Sadly, I learned that I was not supposed to suggest anything that was creative; instead, the real mission was to ensure that all "creative" executions were "on strategy". This job and subsequent corporate assignments contributed to sending my creative side into a deep recession.

In April, 1993, I was in mid-town Manhattan at an advertising agency meeting when I received a call. I was instructed not to go back to work downtown: The World Trade Center was being bombed. After this event, our firm's offices relocated to the north of Boston. On facing the challenge of having to adapt to Boston after living in New York and Hong Kong, I decided to make an even more significant change and left the big-city life behind. The coastline of Gloucester beckoned to me and so I bought a property there and began a new chapter in my life, in more ways than one. I met my husband on the day I closed on my house, but that is its own story. For now, suffice to say, his world was that of a master craftsman, which is a world without the structure and boundaries of corporate America and where creativity in all its forms reigns. His customers call him "Michaelangelo".

Fast-forward to 1999, which is when I embraced married life. Among the subjects we both loved were history and collecting old glass. Sea glass was plentiful right across from our new home on the water. I found that my creative side was tugging at me, especially as I sat and listened to my husband play the piano every night. My husband did not want to talk about business or marketing, he wanted me to join him in artistic expression. Oh my, what should I do?

Consequently, I tried piano lessons again, but it was too little too late! My husband plays by ear whereas I had to learn by numbers, so it was no fun at all. Then I started to think, what could I do with this crazy growing collection of sea glass? There were many artists working with sea glass already but, unlike them, I was not a trained artist. Thinking like a marketer, however, I hit upon a niche idea, one that was literally part of my daily routine: hair accessories. There was a gap in this segment of the market as hair jewelry was a lost art-form. Thus, "Beach Glass Barrettes" was born, a brand I created that evolved into "Cape Ann Designs". I stress that this is a business, *not* a hobby. My hobbies are golf, tennis, kayaking, and other activities that no one will *ever* pay me to do! As for my hair accessories, my husband loved the work and my designs right from the start; it had a huge positive impact on our relationship and he has been my muse and best advocate ever since.

When I first dived into the sea glass artistry phenomenon, I found that, while I was "late to the party", due to my business acumen and reputation I was invited to join in. A group of artists approached me to help them put on the first-ever "Sea Glass Festival" in the area. My involvement did not stop there; next, they asked me to join the board of the sponsoring arts collaborative seARTS. From here, I organized the jewelers in our town, inviting them to participate in art shows and encouraging other

GEM 32

artists who made "wearable art" to join in as well. We changed our name to "The Wearable Art Group".

After five years of successfully running free community shows and events, we took a huge leap in 2011 and launched a runway show to showcase wearable art and promote it among the art-buying audience. A local editor reported, "On a Sunday afternoon in autumn, Gloucester's customarily genteel Bass Rocks Golf Club was invaded by a creative force so strong as to stretch the bounds of the imagination of even the most imaginative." By 2017, we had progressed from taking 2.5 days to sell $9K of wearable art, to selling $18K-worth in 1.5 hours. At our fundraiser last year, we cleared $35K.

In the process, I have managed to build a reputation as a leader in the arts community and am a juried member of the Cape Ann Artisans Open Studios, the oldest open studio tour in the country. Currently, I am spinning off an arts marketing coaching and consulting practice.

In my jewelry design business, I use all of my marketing skills and newly acquired artistic skills. This works nicely alongside my cyclical consulting practice, which focuses on helping business-to-business service and technology companies grow through marketing and ecosystem building. Does one feed the other? Absolutely! Today we live in a world where storytelling wins the day. Creative endeavors make your personal story rich, inviting, and human.

Think about it: When was the last time someone showed sincere interest in discussing your "sales pipeline" or "cash flow" at a cocktail party?

Visit me at: *(www.MarketingRecon.com* and *www.CapeAnnDesigns.com).*

◆ ◆ ◆

GEM 32

Gem 32 Essayist: **Jacqueline M. Ganim-DeFalco**
Business Advisor and Founder, Marketing Recon

Jacqueline Ganim-DeFalco is a marketing and business advisor who builds ecosystems for clients to power new market development and business growth. She built her professional foundation in the telecommunications sector and continues to work in the technology and service sectors. In 1998, Jacqueline launched Marketing Recon.

Jacqueline has worked on assignments that involve new market development, product launches, partner programs, and value proposition testing using her "marketing reconnaissance" approach to research and evaluate business growth alternatives. She has also led several well recognized industry wide collaborations for the software sector focused on Open Source and Cloud Computing.

Jacqueline holds an B.A. from Emory University, an MBA in International Business/Marketing from Stern (NYU) and completed the International Management Program at the University of International Business and Economics in Beijing, China (1987). Among her positions at NYNEX, she served as Managing Director in Asia; Director of Advertising for the NYNEX Yellow Pages' during its award winning years, and led internet marketing and partnerships in the early days of the World Wide Web. She led the GTE Interactive Business Marketing group for two years before forming her own advisory practice.

Jacqueline resides in Gloucester, MA with her husband. She has served on local community boards including the Cape Ann YMCA and was the Chair of the Society for the Encouragement of the Arts. Her sea glass art work is featured in C.S. Lambert's Passion for Sea Glass and she is a juried member of the Cape Ann Artisans. In addition to creating sea glass jewelry, she sought to raise the bar for the category and formed a Wearable Art Group in 2007. In 2011, the group launched "Celebrate Wearable Art, a runway event. It has grown to be a well-loved, professional regional showcase of the art for the body.

GEM 32

GEM 33

This I know for sure:
When you are trying to make it in the music business, you can't rush the process.

Young people like myself, hear the music, appreciate the lifestyle associated with it, and being completely ignorant about the industry, believe that it's easy to make it in the music business because we are "special" and passionate. This is the very definition of "ignorance is bliss."

Having no family or friends in the music industry, I had no natural path into it and no knowledge about its inner workings. This didn't stop me from blissfully diving in –with my only asset being a belief in myself. What I believed in was my ability to deeply reflect on life and to put my words into song like connecting pieces of a puzzle. I had to develop my own GPS as a guide for where to go and how to get there in the music business, however.

This is where passion comes into play; it's the trusted inner voice that guides you through the unexplored forest and the unfamiliar with a belief that "it will all work out." You know you love something when there's no reasonable explanation for why you do it. In the beginning, my desire to pursue a career in music was not validated or encouraged by anyone. It was only me, myself, and I in the club of thinking doing so was a good idea.

Even though I was my own cheerleading squad and in a blissful state, I could never have imagined how long it would take me to get where I am today, which is not to say that "I have made it." I am in the space where I have finally learned how to perform on stage, how to get gigs, and how to captivate audiences when I am on stage. Sometimes, I even get paid.

My present position in the music business is evidence of having come a long way, but it is not where I thought I'd be. When I graduated from high school at 18, I just knew that I'd be signed to major record label within three months. Boy was I wrong! When I finally got into a recording studio, I found that I wasn't as great as I thought I was either; I lacked confidence and sounded robotic as if I was reading the lyrics, which I was. This was a "wake-up call." Had I just spent money for a recording session that I wasn't happy with? Yes, I did. Worse, I hated the sound of my voice primarily because I didn't sound like my favorite artist after all. Hum?

I didn't have a great experience when I performed before a live audience for the first time either when I was 18 years old. My brother still jokes about it to this day. It was caught on camera, so we still look at it and laugh. The problem was that I lacked movement on stage, didn't know how to engage the audience, and exhibited a host of other limitations. Hum?

After countless disappointments I began to consider that perhaps I wasn't a performer after all and that I might be better off just being a songwriter. I had many conversations with family and friends who advised me to develop and launch Plan B for my life and to stop chasing the dream. Privately, I got more and more depressed as I realized how much time and money I was spending and not getting anywhere. And, the little money I was able to spend wasn't nearly enough and didn't put a dent in how much was needed to be in the business of music. It was becoming increasingly difficult socially as well. Everybody constantly asked me, "how is the music coming?" Sometimes I was able to fake it and reply with a positive response but inside I was scared and filled with anxiety.

Worse yet, I didn't want to invite people whom I knew to attend any of my performances because I was ashamed of them and the venues in which I was performing. Despite how bad some of the venues were, I had to pay to perform in them.

Naturally, I had to face reality and ask myself: "why isn't music happening for me, what am I doing wrong?" I constantly compared myself to established artists, both consciously and subconsciously, and tried to make my songs sound like theirs but it didn't work. It wasn't until I reached the age of 23 that I finally started to feel comfortable in my style and in the recording studio. When I finally felt proud of myself, I invited family and friends to attend my performances.

Finally, I was getting a little traction. By the time I was 25 years old, I plunged in and performed at an "open mic" venue called "World Cafe Live." The demographics of the audience were different than in my previous venues and was a step up. Amazingly, it didn't cost the performer to perform at the "open mic", whereas previously I had been paying to do so at really shabby places. This is an example of what happens when you have no one to show you the way; you have to learn by doing and by trial and error.

Things were beginning to look up. My material was getting better and so was I as a performer. When I received applause before completing my songs for the first time, it was a real breakthrough moment and I felt like the movie "Rudy" when Sean Astin finally receives his acceptance letter to Notre Dame.

GEM 33

I was now just a little higher up on the ladder but with a long way to go. With some validation, I felt ready to meet with fellow artists to see how we could collaborate. One artist, an electric guitarist, agreed to give me a try and since then we have performed together ever since. On my part, I have improved by making a commitment to memorize every word of my songs and have strengthened my vocal abilities to the point that I no longer need a vocal track to play alongside of me as accompaniment.

Ten years into the game, I now have a following and a defined style. People around Philly know my name (Monte') and come to see me at the various venues where I am now booked. The host from the previous "open mic" venue took an interest in me and now books me at acclaimed venues across the city. When I say I get bookings, that means I GET PAID. Wow, finally. When I hear the sound of the applause, I know that my hunch was right: I do have talent. Each month, there is a showcase at "World Cafe Live" and after winning against other talented artists, I have been invited to perform at the major annual showcase, which is a big deal.

I am on the move and on the path. I haven't made it, but am making it, slowly but surely. As the process ensues, I have learned not to rush it because I can't even if I tried. The best thing to do is to enjoy the journey and not leave all of the happiness for the final destination. I think this applies to everyone's journey.

✦ ✦ ✦

Gem 33 Essayist: **Rudy Monteiro**

Rudolph A. Monteiro, known by his stage name "Monte", was born and raised in Germantown, Philadelphia. He recalls first becoming interested in hip-hop after stumbling across the debut album from Nas "Illmatic" – while working on his brother's computer to complete a school project. It was a completely new sound to him even though the album was now 10 years old at the time. It stood out easily from the modern music he was used to listening to at the time. From then on, he sought out music that was of this genre and epoch. "It was like taking a history lesson that was enjoyable."

Not long after being drawn to the music of Nas, and to music of that era, Monte' began writing rap songs. He hesitantly recited these to a selective few friends. This surprised those who heard them. They encouraged him to share them more widely, but at the time, he was too shy to do so. Eventually and gradually, however, he broke out of his shell. In the process, Monte' took a greater interest in his English classes in school and was particularly eager to be poetic at every opportunity.

Over the years, Monte's writing style has taken many forms and continues to evolve. He enjoys storytelling the most because the themes involved transcend time and are relatable to listener over time. Monte' has performed at many venues across Philadelphia and takes pride in staying pristine and fresh for every new crowd. His "gigs" include shows such as "Love Fest" at World Cafe Live; "The Hype" at Bourbon and Branch; and the "Spoken Word" campaign of State Representative Steve Kinsey; among others. You can currently find his music on all streaming platforms including Spotify and Apple Music under such projects as "Monte 2 AM", as well as "Monte For The Love".

GEM 1

Afterword

This I know for sure (so far):

I want adults to do things today that will help the world be a better place tomorrow for young people like myself.

My name is Negash Gebre. I am only eleven years old. I mostly have questions so far, but I also see a lot of things. My Mom (Sharon Freeman) and Dad (Peter Hagos Gebre) try to protect me from the news and bad things in the world, but they can't. I see television, in limited doses, and get news in all forms—from the radio, games, the Internet, and from other kids in school.

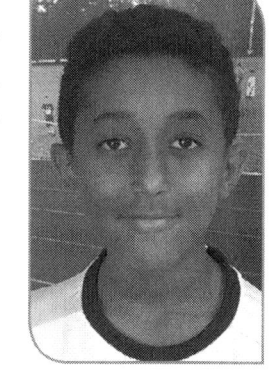

Some of what I see makes me happy and excited about the future—things like robots and going to outer space. Some things make me scared, like school shootings and contagious diseases. When I heard about Ebola, for instance, it terrorized me and I still mention the word Ebola every day, wondering whether something will make me catch it. Then, there are the many questions that I have about stuff I see that doesn't seem to make any sense. When I watch television and see commercials about a particular medicine and hear all of the bad things the medicine will do, I ask my parents: "Why do people take that then?

My Mom has read some of the "This I know for sure" messages in this book to me and I understand that they are giving really good advice; I just hope that people listen to it so kids like me don't have to worry so much about the future.

When I study so hard every day and practice so many sports, I am doing it in the hope that by the time I grow up, I can be great and the world will be great too.

I hope everyone can be happy and get along and that my generation—and those after me—will have a chance to make our dreams come true!

✦ ✦ ✦

33 GEMS
Wisdom for Living Pieces of Life's Puzzle

Made in the USA
Middletown, DE
23 September 2018